Time Management at Work

How to Maximize Productivity at Work and in Life

Dave Young

Table of Contents

Table of Contents

Chapter 1 - What Is Time Management?

"Time isn't the main thing. It's the only thing." - Miles Davis

Time is your most precious resource, but are you utilizing it to the utmost? We all have 24 hours in a day, but it's how you use those hours that determines your productivity — and ultimately, your success.

Have you ever wondered why some people get more work done, reach more goals, and still have time to pursue their hobbies? The answer is simple: by managing their time well.

In today's fast-paced world, time management is a prized skill. With this ability, you have enough time to accomplish everything without succumbing to pressure.

Time management is the way you utilize each minute. It refers to organizing your day according to your priorities and values. It also determines how much time you spend on certain activities.

Time management includes, but is not limited to, effective planning and task prioritization. A good time manager sets realistic deadlines, goals, and objectives.

If done right, it allows you to complete tasks and achieve goals despite any challenges that may arise. Your efficiency will lead you on the path of success.

This skill not only has the potential to increase your productivity but also has an impact on your well-being. If you take care of everything ahead of time, your stress levels go down considerably.

Time is finite. Once you spend your minutes, hours, and days, they are gone. You can't buy, beg, borrow, or steal more time. So, to maximize your effectiveness and efficiency, it is necessary to manage tasks according to their priorities.

Time is money. People who get hourly wages or who bill clients by the hour know this truth intimately. To ensure they are on the road to success, companies make sure they manage time effectively. This includes prioritizing ruthlessly, making it easier to take on new opportunities yet sustain growth.

Time management sounds straightforward, but it is not easy to accomplish. If your schedule is jam-packed but you're still not getting the desired results, you're probably not doing it right.

Remember: being busy is not equivalent to being effective.

Why It Matters

Effective time management can help you control your day, working through both your work life and private life. There's a misconception that time management is only applicable to the professional realm. However, this skill also allows you to reach personal goals and streamline household tasks.

There are a variety of tools and apps that claim to help you manage time better. You can note your tasks on your to-do list and arrange your sleep schedule. But, unless you understand the importance of managing time, these strategies won't work as well as they should.

Time management may seem monotonous. After all, following the same schedule every day can get on your nerves. However, time management is a necessary life skill that everyone needs to have.

The benefits of developing time management skills are endless. They can drastically improve all areas of your life. If done wisely, you will see an increase in your work performance.

How often have you put off finishing a task, then ended up rushing to get it done a few hours before the deadline, leaving yourself stressed and fatigued both mentally and physically? Good time management ensures you don't have to go through either.

The top 4 reasons why effective time management matters are, that it:

Allows You to Meet Deadlines

Deadlines help you to accomplish tasks according to their importance. They motivate people to focus on the task at hand and adjust their pace when needed. Workers need to know when a project is expected.

Time management helps you manage your workload in a way that maximizes your performance without sacrificing your health. When you allow every task a fixed schedule, you condition your brain into thinking it needs to be completed within that period.

When you have a realistic schedule, it allows you to get the best possible work performance and a better outcome.

Improves the Quality of Your Work

Prioritizing tasks according to their importance is an effective way to improve the quality of your work. Your performance can suffer when you are worried about a looming deadline. On the contrary, when you're not pressed for time, your performance is much better. You can give the task the attention and effort it deserves.

As an employee, your work reflects on your company and its quality standards. By giving adequate time to each task, you complete the project while ensuring the quality of work is not compromised in any way.

Make sure each project has a realistic time frame so that you do not end up rushing things. Completing work before the deadline allows you to squeeze in any changes required without the pressure of time constraints.

Eliminates Work Stress

To maintain a healthy work-life balance, it is important to manage your time accordingly. We're familiar with the stress brought on by trying to juggle multiple responsibilities.

Putting a lot of thought into your work schedule will help you be more relaxed. When you know that tasks are scheduled properly, you avoid the stress brought on by missed deadlines or enormous workloads.

Time management puts you in control of your life. You are free to schedule tasks according to their respective priorities. Completing your task according to the time allotted is an efficient way to avoid stress.

One strategy is to do difficult tasks first, preferably when you are not burdened by other responsibilities. Once this is out of the way, you no longer have to spend time worrying about it.

Increases Professional Opportunities

Managing your time with basic everyday tools like the calendar and to-do list will take you a long way. Good time management enables you to complete tasks faster, leaving you with free time to learn and excel at work.

This spike in productivity and efficiency will help you focus, boost your confidence, and open you to more career opportunities. When you manage your time well, you will soon earn an excellent reputation at work. Remember, punctuality and efficiency are two essential traits that lead to that coveted promotion.

The Need for Time Management in a World That's Short for Time

We live in a world that's driven by technology. Humanity continues to invent tools and processes that will help us do more, faster. But why does it feel like the average worker has less free time than ever before?

There is also no shortage of blogs, books, podcasts, and apps that claim to help you manage time better. However, most of the time, they don't work at all.

Time management may look like a universal concept, but the application differs from person to person. We're all unique when it comes to our skill sets, jobs, and private lives. By generalizing, we're undermining ourselves.

What works is learning about basic time management skills and principles. Then, trying them out in real life. Some will give you an unbelievable boost in productivity, while others will be duds. Once you figure this out, you can customize a time management strategy that suits your personality and lifestyle.

This endeavor may seem like a waste of time initially, using valuable hours that you could've spent doing the task instead. But in the long run, you'll be grateful you spent time doing it.

Time cannot be tampered with, but our schedules can be enhanced. Here are some skills that will help you utilize time to your advantage.

Make a To-Do List

This, by far, is the simplest and the most effective strategy. Lists can help you remember things. Writing things down frees you from the responsibility of having to remember everything, which is a big advantage. A lighter mental load gives you the space to construct ideas and stretch your creativity.

You don't have to go all-in immediately with a long list of everything you need to accomplish for the year. Start with smaller, achievable goals. A five-item checklist, all of which get ticked off by the end of the day, is better than a 20-item list, as the latter will overwhelm you.

By creating a to-do list, you ensure that all your tasks are compiled in one place, and nothing slips through the cracks.

Also, don't make the mistake of checking your progress every few minutes. This will just bring on unnecessary stress.

Prioritize Ruthlessly

After you create a list, make sure to put the most important tasks at the top. This will help you manage them faster instead of going about it haphazardly. Note that it is crucial to factor in the most pressing tasks of the day. What are the three major things that will help you succeed?

When setting goals to be accomplished, remember, not everything is important. Make sure you only put important tasks there, not just busywork. Spending time on less important tasks will get in the way of your progress. Don't forget, being busy and being productive are not the same thing.

Are you prioritizing what truly matters? Follow Eisenhower's matrix. Also referred to as Urgent-Important Matrix, it is a framework for prioritization and time management of daily tasks, designed to optimize productivity. The matrix helps you sort through tasks on the basis of their urgency and importance. It helps you zero in on the less urgent tasks which you can then consider delegating or not doing at all. It was invented by Dwight D. Eisenhower, the 34th President of the United States.

According to the matrix, just because something is needed immediately does not mean that it should take precedence. Completing the important and urgent tasks on the list will ensure you have enough time to go through the other, less-important tasks.

When you prioritize tasks, you ensure that they have your undivided attention and focus. This will improve the quality of your work.

Prioritizing also prevents multitasking. While a tempting option, multitasking does more harm than good. When you switch your attention, you end up doing both tasks haphazardly. Instead of excelling at one activity, multitasking reduces your productivity in both.

Set Attainable Goals

Setting realistic goals can help maximize productivity and efficiency. Goals should be attainable and realistic. Setting unrealistic expectations will be counter-productive and stress-inducing. It will burn you out.

A specific goal is always more attainable, so make sure you don't set one that's too broad. A clear goal means you know exactly how to measure your success. It is one of the best practices in your personal or professional life.

Know what your goals are, how much time they require to be accomplished, what level of priority they hold, and allot the required time to it. Most importantly, see it through. You cannot add more hours to a day, but you can map out tasks during times when you have more energy and focus.

Setting goals as part of managing time is an essential element of success. Goals provide clear direction so that everyone is on the same page. This makes it easier to assess the workload and allocate resources where needed.

Avoid Procrastination

Procrastination is the bane of our existence. The multitude of distractions available have only been increasing with the rise in technology. We have a plethora of apps and activities that are bound to take our attention away from the important tasks at hand. So, if you're looking to achieve maximum productivity, you'll have to put away your habit of procrastinating.

Remember, more than a time management issue, procrastination is an emotional management issue. Procrastination is sometimes brought on by a fear of failure. Therefore, remember to celebrate your achievements, however small, and reward yourself for them.

Procrastination is a threat to productivity that can affect even the best workers on a team. However, breaking your goals into small tasks can help you overcome this habit. You'll be less tempted to delay a five-minute activity than a five-hour one. It's also a good idea to set critical and time-consuming tasks during your hours of peak productivity.

Avoiding procrastination can help you boost your self-control, hit more milestones, and tap into your potential.

Delegate Tasks

Are you the type who prefers to work alone? Perhaps you are afraid others won't pull their weight or meet your expectations. For your well-being, it is important not to overload yourself.

Delegation is sometimes seen as admitting weakness, that you cannot complete the tasks allotted to you. But some tasks require the help of others on your team. Thus, it becomes important to sort your tasks and assign some of them to your colleagues.

Delegating tasks will ensure their completion without putting the pressure of a looming deadline on one individual. Plus, you leverage the unique strengths and skills of everyone on your team. If you are poor in math, it might be a good idea to delegate the budget to a colleague who has a background in accounting.

Avoid micromanaging once you've assigned the responsibility to a specific person. However, make sure they are still accountable to you and the team.

It is never too late to start working on your time management skills. It will not only enable you to have an efficient workday but will also enhance the overall quality of your life.

Wouldn't it be great to have time enough for everything you love?

Chapter 2 - What Happens When There Is No Time Management?

"The great dividing line between success and failure can be expressed in five words - 'I did not have time'." - Franklin Field

Not getting work done on time can be extremely frustrating. No matter how you rearrange your day, it seems like an impossible dream to finish everything that's on your plate.

You know you have what it takes to deliver. You have all the skills and experience you need, but despite your best efforts, you still keep missing your deadlines. Or, if you crunch and get things done, it is at the cost of your health and relationships.

You might be tempted to compare your workload with that of your colleague. Perhaps you think that your boss is being unfair or unrealistic. But the problem goes deeper than that.

It's not them. It's not you either. It's just a lack of proper time management.

When you have zero time management skills, you tend to take things as they come. This is the worst thing you could do when you're looking for career advancement.

Without time management, you'll always be short for time. It will always seem like your 24-hour day is not enough for work, sleep, exercise, and recreation. You may end up doing high-priority tasks at the last possible moment which gives you no opportunity to make necessary changes or enhancements. You end up disappointing your boss, your clients, and yourself.

If you think time management does not have an impact on business, think again. Companies rely on their employees to take care of certain tasks within a specific time frame. Failure to do so can potentially reduce profits and damage client relationships. Losing customers' trust is detrimental to the success of any business, big or small.

The effects of poor time management skills go way beyond the four walls of your office. It could affect your relationships, lower your self-esteem, and give you a negative outlook on life.

Consequences of Poor Time Management

Lower Productivity

You can get away with not having time management skills for a while. But eventually, it will start to affect your productivity. Your output decreases and the quality of your work goes downhill.

Poor time managers are likely to be less efficient at work. A lot of people think that just because they're working around the clock, they're being productive. That's far from the truth.

Completing your tasks in haste means you're not giving them the necessary time and attention. You end up cutting corners and compromising on quality.

Attempting to start a project with unclear priorities and no proper schedule can be detrimental to your productivity. Any discrepancy or emergency that arises can affect your progress.

Without time management, you are more likely to prioritize unnecessary, yet urgent projects. By the time you start working on more valuable tasks, you've already exhausted yourself. You've lost so much time and energy, so you can no longer give it your best shot.

The key to high productivity is knowing what needs your immediate attention and getting it done first. Good time management ensures you allocate your time and resources to what matters most.

Missed Deadlines

A lack of time management skills makes it twice as difficult to complete a task. You're often unsure how long it takes to do things.

When external factors come into play, it becomes easier to shift the blame.

"There were too many tasks at hand."

"I was busy all day."

"My children kept interrupting me."

But are others truly at fault?

You keep on failing to meet deadlines because you don't plan.

The problem lies in not setting a time limit for each task. We tend to underestimate how much time it takes to do our work. This can result in allotting more time to one task and less to another when the reverse would have been better.

Projects are often broken down into smaller tasks. Any hindrance in the first task can impede the progress of the succeeding tasks. Soon, there's a domino effect that delays your deliverables and affects your entire team.

Increased Work Stress

Are you always in a rush at work? We've all been there.

Poor time management is almost always the number one cause of work stress. You get panicky and lose focus. Your anxiety reaches an all-time high when you cannot manage the workload efficiently.

Without proper time management, you often feel overwhelmed by the seemingly endless list of deadlines.

Workplace stress has become a badge of honor in the corporate world. The ever-increasing competition between companies and the ensuing need to catch up to the others has led to heavier workloads and extended office hours, leading to stress.

Unfortunately, stress harms your health, both physically and mentally.

However, a bit of planning and strategy are all you need to keep stress at bay. Treat the cause, not the symptoms.

Time management is crucial to control work stress. When we have a lot of work on our hands, we tend to get anxious over looming deadlines. We're unable to focus our thoughts and formulate a clear plan that best suits our schedule.

Poor time management means you don't have enough time for all your projects and tasks. On the other hand, effective time management can easily eradicate this problem and help you lead a stress-free work life.

Poor Professional Reputation

Companies look for employees who can attract more clients and bring in repeat business. This is possible only when employees have a well-planned schedule and excel in time management skills.

When clients pay you, they expect quality work, but if you fail to do so, you end up losing your clients to another provider.

No one wants to work with a company that's unreliable, unprofessional, and untrustworthy. If you miss deadlines or deliver mediocre results, it tarnishes your employer's reputation.

An employee with poor time management skills becomes a liability. No workforce would cheer at the inclusion of such a person, knowing full well they're going to hinder the overall progress.

Poor time management can hurt your professional reputation and decrease your chances of getting promoted.

Remember, companies value people who consistently deliver as promised. This is why good time management is vital if you wish to excel professionally.

No Work-Life Balance

A lack of time management skills leads to zero work-life balance. Work should not be the be-all and end-all of your existence. Sure, you must earn a salary to pay for living expenses, but there is more to life than work.

Ideally, our work-life should only constitute 8 hours of the day. With no management skills, this seems impossible.

But with time management, you can reach an equilibrium between your personal and professional priorities. While it is important to have an efficient work life, it is equally important to have time for your relationships and self-care.

With poor time management skills, we find ourselves holding the short end of the stick, with no time for recreation, hobbies, or socializing.

Because we don't prioritize our tasks according to their importance, we end up doing them outside our working hours, utilizing time we could've been spent with family or close friends.

Work-life balance can only be achieved when you take control of your time.

Lost Money

When we're in a hurry, we tend to spend more on conveniences and ready-made items. You end up paying for things that you could do yourself if you only had the time.

Instead of spending hours preparing healthy home-cooked meals, an employee willingly shells out hundreds of dollars on fast food and takeout. A harried office worker may outsource laundry, house cleaning, gardening, etc.

This frees up time and allows you to stay longer in the office.

Take note that in some cases, it makes sense to pay for such services. Childcare, for example, is a necessity for professional parents. When you live far from urban centers, owning a car is often safer and faster than taking public transportation. If you need a mental health break, a housekeeper may be a godsend.

But for most people, it becomes a vicious cycle. These conveniences are so expensive that you end up working overtime to be able to afford them. The money spent could have gone into savings instead.

Poor time management has an impact on your finances in other ways. Think about all the late fees, missed reservations, expired discount coupons, and wasted gym memberships. If these things had been on your calendar, you could have saved a lot of money and enjoyed what you would have already paid for.

Challenges in the Modern Workplace: What Distracts Us the Most

There's no shortage of devices, activities, and things around us. We are working harder and putting in more work than previous generations, but we also have twice as many distractions.

Why are distractions so harmful? Whether you're working at home, at a nearby café, or in the office, distractions abound. And while it doesn't take much time to get distracted, it takes quite some time for our brain to regain focus after — 25 minutes to be exact.

That 5-minute social media break can easily cost you a couple more hours at work.

The way we work is entwined with new developments in technology. The modern workplace is fragile and agile, and in a lot of instances, virtual. It connects people with varying skill sets across the globe.

While automation has made this possible, boosting businesses and increasing productivity alongside, it also has various drawbacks - primarily more distractions.

Workplace distractions don't just affect your work, they affect your health too. Getting interrupted often leads to stress, which has proven psychological and physiological symptoms.

How do you manage these distractions before they become an issue? You start by identifying your problem areas.

Here are some of the common distractions found in the workplace:

Mobile Phones

Are you often distracted? Your smartphone is probably the culprit. It's both a boon and a bane.

Most people feel a pressure to always be available on social media. Since this has become the norm, it is not surprising that this is the major cause of distraction in the workplace.

A lot of companies have started putting the "no phone while working" clause in their contracts to prevent this. However, some employees need to use their mobile phones — say, a social media manager or a person who does fieldwork.

The personal use of mobile phones should be limited. While companies understand the need to stay updated, it's difficult to moderate the use of mobiles at work. Texting, calling, and browsing the internet can be super addictive.

Constantly checking your phone at work can decrease productivity; you tend to lose focus and commit more errors when you are distracted.

While it may seem inconsequential, this habit could potentially lose the company a lot of money.

Interruptions

Interruptions may seem innocent, but they have the potential to lessen your productivity. Your colleague could pop in to ask a question or drop by to say "Hi" when they clock-in. Your spouse could be asking what you want for dinner. Your children could open your home office door every 15 minutes in a bid for attention.

Take note that conversations among colleagues help build healthy relationships. But if done excessively, these interruptions tend to interfere with our flow state, when we're most productive. The little seconds of interruptions can set you back a long way.

How do you deal with these supposedly harmless interruptions?

Consider adding a dedicated hour for taking questions, solving issues, and checking on your work colleagues. If you have a closed office, put a "Do not disturb" sign on the door.

If you work in an open-plan office, invest in noise-canceling headphones; better yet just politely tell people that you're busy.

Workplaces that have minimal distractions are known to be more progressive. This allows employees to feel more focused and self-fulfilled. It's a win-win.

Disorganized Space

A disorganized workspace increases your anxiety and stress. For one thing, the sight of all that junk can be distracting. It can affect your focus and limit your ability to process information.

This also explains why people who work from home prefer a virtual background during video calls instead of keeping it real.

It is also why a lot of employees prefer keeping their web cameras turned off.

It is important to organize your work area every week or so. If you don't pay attention, your clutter can end up consuming your entire desk.

A little clutter probably won't hurt, but that little pile of paper can soon turn into a mountain. Eventually, it will take you 15 minutes to find an important document in all the clutter.

To combat this problem, learn to declutter. Get rid of anything that you no longer need. Then, put away everything that is not of immediate use to you. Use technology to your advantage. As far as possible, store information through electronic means.

If you still need paperwork, make sure there aren't any individual sheets scattered around. Make sure everything is filed properly. Applying the one-touch method (touch the item only once to then open, read, respond, & file) will keep your organization task much simpler.

Multitasking

Working on two tasks at the same time may seem like killing two birds with one stone, but this couldn't be any farther from the truth. Instead, multitasking hinders your progress, focus, and productivity.

When you task-switch, you put more pressure on your brain to keep up. This split attention affects your performance in both tasks. You end up constantly shuffling through your to-do list and doing substandard work, leading to even bigger backlogs.

You not only leave all the tasks unfinished, but you also end up spending more time on them combined than what you would have spent working on them individually.

Meetings

Frequent meetings are a drain on time and energy. During a busy day, the last thing you need is to attend a meeting when you can use that time on something more productive instead.

While unclear goals and agendas are the primary drivers for unproductive meetings, employees end up losing a substantial number of working hours that could otherwise have been gainfully utilized. They're instructed to drop whatever task they're working on to attend meetings that may not help them meet individual goals. Because this disrupts the workflow, it becomes increasingly difficult to regain that focus once the meeting is over.

Therefore, consider sending emails or texts to the concerned personnel instead of holding meetings that require everyone to be present.

Background Noise

Background noise may seem inconsequential, but it can lower your level of productivity. Between noisy co-workers, constantly buzzing mobile phones, the din coming from outside the office, and running machines, noise can affect your focus and memory.

Statistics reveal that more than half the office population admitted to being distracted by background noise. Given how much effort it takes to refocus your attention, this is nothing short of a disaster.

Some people work better with ambient noise. But when a project requires total attention, it is best to relocate to a quieter place or invest in noise-canceling headphones.

Developing High Performance: How to Improve Your Focus at Work

Time management may seem simple, but it's not something you can learn in a day. It requires discipline, an understanding of your goals, knowing your limitations, and being aware of the workload assigned to you.

Increasing your productivity is not something that can be done on a whim. It is a basic outcome of good time management skills.

We've all been in a position where we found it difficult to focus on the task at hand, thereby undermining our performance. Working in a noisy and distracting world can lead to stress, irritation, and frustration.

Your ability to focus on a task until completion is a good indicator of success. Boosting your concentration will open opportunities for career advancement.

Staying on task may not seem like a big deal. Perhaps you possess the skill set required. But if you're constantly surrounded by distractions, completing a project can be a Herculean task.

The good news is that you can improve your focus. It's like a mental muscle - the more you work on it, the stronger it gets. However, it requires real effort. You may have to make major changes in your habit, but it will be worth it.

To achieve professional goals, you must be intentional about planning your day, eliminating needless tasks, and prioritizing the important ones. This will result in a good outcome for both you and your employer.

Let us look at a couple of strategies to enhance your focus and amp up your productivity.

Set Personal Deadlines

When creating a to-do list, make sure you mark all the tasks that require immediate attention. Highlight the high-priority ones or rank them in descending order.

Deadlines are a good way to ensure you get your work done on time. In addition to scheduling your tasks according to the deadlines set by your superior, make sure you set personal deadlines as well.

If a task is supposed to be submitted by 8:00 p.m., aim to complete it by 6:00 p.m. This will give you extra time to recheck, make edits, and take care of any last-minute changes.

It is always wise to complete a task a couple of days before its submission.

Setting personal deadlines may seem like you're putting in too much time for what-ifs. But what if you suddenly have a malfunctioning computer, or an internet connectivity problem, or a sick day? You can still get the work done on time despite these complications.

Compartmentalize

Your ability to compartmentalize is one of the most important skills for success. Compartmentalizing allows you to divide your tasks and responsibilities into different time slots spread across several days. This ensures your tasks don't overlap and cause unnecessary stress.

Compartmentalizing is simple. It involves putting each task or priority in its own mental "box." You should only focus on one box at a time. You need to discard everything else except for the single task in front of you.

It will take time, but you can learn to mentally "turn off" tasks until you are ready to see them through. Initially, you will need to control outside factors, including turning off your mobile phone or finding a quiet place to work.

Compartmentalizing is considered a coping mechanism because it helps decrease stress levels.

Monotask

Monotasking is all about giving your undivided attention to one thing. Also called single tasking, it is the opposite of multitasking.

Contrary to popular misconceptions, multitasking is not a skill set that leads to productivity. Research suggests that multitasking can make you work less efficiently.

When it comes to working, doing less is more. When you monotask, you minimize the chances of making errors. This leads to better and consistent results, fast.

When you pay more attention to one task, you will have better results compared to juggling several tasks simultaneously.

Practice Mindfulness

Mindfulness is all about being fully aware of the moment, including the task you're working on. Here, your brain can be your worst enemy. It tends to reminisce, daydream — anything but focus on the present.

While it's not easy to stop your mind from wandering, you can improve your ability to focus through mindful meditation. However, mindfulness is not limited to meditation. It's a state of mind.

You start by conditioning your mind to focus on an exercise, like paying attention to your breathing. When your attention starts to wander, bring it back to the exercise. This may seem boring at first, but you'll soon notice that this exercise will strengthen your mental discipline. It will also increase your focus and enhance learning and memory.

Take Mental Breaks

How many times have you worked on a boring task and found it went on and on and on? We tend to push ourselves without taking a break. It's as if we're convinced that taking a break would hinder our progress.

However, a rest period is highly recommended. Taking a mental break during a tedious workday will fuel your creativity. It will give your brain time to recharge, and rest will help you focus better and retain more information.

Working nonstop can have adverse effects on your physical and mental health, and it can potentially wear you down physically and mentally as well.

When you feel fatigue setting in, take some time off to reset your brain. You can use this break to take a walk, listen to music, meditate, stretch, or have a short power nap. Do something that fuels your motivation.

Organize Your Workspace

Your productivity is greatly influenced by how your workspace looks. If it's cluttered, rest assured you're not winning the "Most Productive Employee Award" anytime soon.

A neat desk points to an organized and effective worker. Not only that, but this also makes you more efficient. Looking for misfiled documents or missing items is a waste of your precious time.

Some people seem to thrive in chaos, but they are more the exception than the rule.

Keeping your workspace clean may take some time, but it pays off in enhanced focus and productivity. Having a clutter-free workspace can help you think more clearly and produce better results.

Chapter 3 - How to Get Started

"Productivity is never an accident. It is always the result of commitment to excellence, intelligent planning, and focused effort." - Paul J Meyer

We all know someone who is extremely productive. You probably admire:

- a boss who's spearheading several projects while serving on the board of a nonprofit organization
- a neighbor who takes care of a young family while running a small business
- a colleague who is working full time while training for a marathon

Not only that, but these successful people also often do all of these things without sacrificing their health or personal relationships.

What's their secret?

These uber-productive people are adept at time management. They know where their priorities lie, what core competencies they possess, and which time slots work best for specific tasks.

They've mastered the art of time management. Sounds difficult, doesn't it?

The good news? Time management is a learnable skill, not a rare talent. Given the right technique and sufficient motivation, anyone can master it.

The hardest part? You need to get started. Taking that first step is, by far, the most challenging aspect of time management. But once you begin, the benefits of managing your time are undeniable.

Effective time management can significantly lower the amount of stress in your life. Not only do you complete tasks before the deadline, but you also get exceptional results. Plus, you have the opportunity to deal with any discrepancies that may arise.

Time management boils down to having a process where you control how much time you spend on a certain activity. Don't worry; it's not a one-size-fits-all approach. You can select a time management technique that best suits your personality and lifestyle.

We cover some of the most popular strategies below:

- Parkinson's Law
- Pomodoro Technique
- Goal Setting
- 18-Minutes Technique
- Domino Reaction Technique
- Getting Things Done (GTD) Technique

Learn more about these tried-and-tested methods and see which one can help you get the most out of your day.

Parkinson's Law

This is more of a principle that underpins all the other techniques. Parkinson's Law is the adage that "work expands to fill the time allotted."

Here's an example:

Your sister is graduating from university, and your family wants to throw her a party to reward her for all her hard work. How much time would you need to prepare for the celebration?

On paper, it should only take two or three days to get everything done. All you need to do is book a caterer, order balloons, buy a cake, and set up the decorations. At most, it should only take a few hours to create and send out the invitations.

If you have a few weeks to prepare, you will be tempted to go all out. That simple to-do list soon expands as you get more ideas. Or you keep putting off some of the tasks to attend to more urgent matters.

Pretty soon, what should have been a three-day project will take two months to complete. That is Parkinson's Law in a nutshell.

As the above example shows, the amount of time you're given to complete a task is the amount of time it should take to complete it. When you set deadlines too far out, you're guaranteeing that it will take you that much time to complete it.

You may think that allocating more time to certain projects will improve their quality. This is not always true. Instead, you end up having more time to procrastinate. When you devote more hours to accomplishing a task, you also tend to experience more stress about completing it. Talk about prolonging the agony.

Can you use Parkinson's Law to your advantage? Yes, you can.

The Secret: Set a Realistic Deadline

At work, you're usually given a deadline to finish a project. Set your mind to complete the task ahead of that deadline. If the project is due in a week, aim to complete it within 4 days instead. Follow your deadline as much as possible.

Be honest. If the project is something you've done before, you probably know how much time it takes to complete it. How many hours did you spend doing the work? How much time was spent on filler tasks? Was there a simpler or faster way of doing the work?

Factor in breaks and delays, but don't give yourself so much leeway that you end up filling the time with unnecessary tasks. Make sure your attention is focused on what's important.

Watch out for the other extreme of not giving enough time to a project. An occasional all-nighter or weekend project may be necessary, especially during peak seasons. But if you are constantly doing overtime or if you end up getting sick, you may want to reset your expectations.

You may also find it difficult to set a personal deadline if:

- You are assigned an unfamiliar task.
- You are working with new people (team, boss, or suppliers).
- You need to use new and complicated tools.
- You are dealing with a lot of variables or constantly changing requirements.
- You are given an unrealistic deadline by your boss or client.

Accept the reality that your work will fill up the allotted schedule and set deadlines accordingly. By accurately estimating the number of hours needed for a task, you will not only save time, but the complexity of the task will also decrease. When you correctly implement Parkinson's Law in your life, you will soon boost your productivity.

Pomodoro Technique

Have you ever been stuck with a tedious task? Do you find yourself battling distractions or a lack of motivation? Even the most exciting job can get boring if you do it non-stop.

Remember, your brain can't sustain a high level of attention for hours on end. It's natural for your focus to wax and wane throughout the workday.

What then is the best way to improve your concentration and get your work done? Look no further than the Pomodoro Technique.

Developed by Francesco Cirillo in the late 1980s, this method breaks down your workday into intervals of 25-minutes with regular breaks of five minutes between each interval. Each interval is called a Pomodoro. After four to five Pomodoros, you allow yourself a longer break of around 15 to 20 minutes.

The name Pomodoro was inspired by the tomato-shaped timer Cirillo used. Upon completion, Pomodoros are recorded. This contributes to a sense of accomplishment while providing raw data for observation and self-learning.

By using this technique, you reduce the impact that interruptions have on your attention and workflow. It helps you achieve maximum productivity by focusing your intent and energy in short sprints.

Did you know that interruptions harm your concentration? Regaining focus takes a lot of time. Every time you get distracted, you prolong the duration of your task.

The Pomodoro Technique helps you work alongside time instead of struggling with it.

Why the Pomodoro Technique Works

It Is Simple and Effective

You don't need fancy tools or complicated plans to practice this technique. Just follow the steps, and you're set.

It's also quite effective. Since assignments or projects are broken down into manageable tasks, they don't seem as overwhelming. Plus, you get an instant sense of accomplishment when you finish each Pomodoro.

It Helps You Manage Distractions

Distractions are deadly to your concentration. When you use the Pomodoro Technique, you'll notice that distractions can wait. They're not completely gone; you're redirecting them to a time when they don't potentially destroy your productive streak.

You can look at memes, but make sure you do that on your break. If a coworker interrupts you, politely tell them that you can talk during your break. Unless it's a life-or-death situation, a 25-minute delay is perfectly reasonable.

Breaks Are Part of Your Workday

The good thing about the Pomodoro Technique is that mental breaks are already part of your workday. You may feel guilty about taking breaks, but your brain needs them.

You'll be less prone to procrastination or slacking off. It's less tempting to extend your rest period when you know that another one is scheduled within the hour.

Don't skip or shorten these breaks. They're there for a reason. Your brain is a muscle, so it also needs to rest. When you're in the gym, do you head straight from the weights to the treadmill? Of course not. You give yourself a breather between each type of exercise. The same principle holds true in the office.

You Can See Your Progress

When going through each task, remember to jot it down on a piece of paper. This will help you track your progress. It's quite fulfilling to check off tasks as you complete them.

You can immediately spot problem areas, see where you're going wrong, and avoid any inconsistency in your workflow.

When you write things down, you leave your brain free to focus on other things instead of being a holding tank for your work. You not only have a report that attests to your work ethic, but you are also more open to ideas and creative thinking.

It Improves Your Health

Working for an extended period is a sure-fire way of getting stressed and sick. If you sit too long, you will suffer from aches in your back, shoulder, head, neck, or wrist. You may also experience eye strain after hours of staring at a screen.

The Pomodoro Technique has your back, quite literally. It requires you to take frequent breaks, so you have time to get up, walk around the office, or stretch. You can use the 5 minutes to take a drink of water, rest your eyes, or have a quick chat with a colleague.

As much as possible, avoid screens when you take your break. Your brain and eyes will thank you. Remember, good health equals better productivity.

How to Follow the Pomodoro Technique

- Break a project into tasks. Make sure that each task or subtask can be completed within a 25-minute interval or Pomodoro.
- Identify the task you want to accomplish.
- Set the Pomodoro timer to 25 minutes.

- Work on a task until the timer rings. Avoid all distractions while doing so.
- Take a 5-minute break.
- Pick another task and repeat the procedure.
- After 4 intervals, take a longer break of 20-30 minutes so your brain can reset and recharge.

How to Get the Most Out of the Pomodoro Technique

Plan Carefully

Before you start working, take time off to carefully curate your tasks. When you write down tasks, pay attention to how many Pomodoros a certain task will take and plan them accordingly.

See how many hours you work and how many Pomodoros you can fit into your day. If you can't finish them all, leave the remaining tasks for the next day.

Any task that takes more than five Pomodoros to complete should be broken down into more manageable tasks to avoid loss of focus.

When it comes to work, quality always comes first. If you're looking to complete all the tasks, both high priority and low, the quality of your work may suffer.

You can tweak this technique to match your preference. If you're someone who likes to get smaller tasks out of the way before focusing on bigger tasks, you can do those first. Keep in mind that you still need to meet the overall deadline.

Identify Mini Tasks

Not all tasks would require 25 minutes. Replying to an email or publishing a blog post may take you a couple of minutes at most.

As a general rule, you need to work during the whole length of the Pomodoro or it won't be counted as a productive session.

Good thing you don't have to limit yourself to one task per Pomodoro. You can group several smaller tasks within a Pomodoro. The key here is to finish one short task *before* you move on to the next. Do not attempt to work on two or more tasks at the same time.

Or, you can list these filler tasks when you plan out your day. Then, if you have extra minutes left before the timer rings, slot in one of these quick tasks.

Experiment with the Timer

A 25-minute Pomodoro followed by a five-minute break may not work for everyone. Some tasks simply can't be done within 25 minutes. It may also not make sense to break some tasks into intervals.

Fortunately, this technique is not set in stone. The principle here is having dedicated periods of intense focus and planned breaks. Try new combinations. You can work for an hour and take a longer break, or you can work for 15 minutes and take a two-minute break to check notifications.

Download an App

Automation makes life easier, and the same applies to the Pomodoro Technique. There are dozens of apps designed for this method. You can choose free or paid apps with varying features for your phone or laptop.

Most of these apps have a tracking system that lets you identify your most productive days and generate weekly reports. They will also remind you to take a break, often with a customizable alert tone. Some of these apps integrate with communication tools, so your colleagues and boss can immediately see when you're busy.

Goal Setting

Do you struggle with completing important tasks within the allocated hours of your workday? Do you feel like you are exhausting yourself without hitting your expected targets?

Setting goals is crucial to achieving success in the workplace. You need to have a clear-cut idea of what you need to accomplish during each workday. Otherwise, you may end up being busy and exhausted, but not productive.

Goal setting is a powerful process. You set a goal you want to accomplish, and then you put all the hard work into it. Once you start goal setting at work, you'll want to incorporate it into other areas of your life. It's an addiction, but the good kind.

How to Set Goals

Effective goal setting isn't just about choosing your end goal; it's also about the cost you're willing to pay to achieve it.

Find Your 'Why'

The key here is to set goals that you truly want to accomplish. Articulate why each goal is important. Does it align with your values? How will it make your life better? Otherwise, you will lack the motivation to continue.

Prioritize

Which goals are more important? Keep in mind that some goals may be prerequisites for other goals. For example, you can't buy a house if you don't have the funds to pay for it.

Determine Your Timeline

Your goals may be short-term (1 to 6 months), medium-term (6 to 18 months), or long-term (18 months and up). Determine if your goal can be quickly achieved or if it would require a longer period. Your goals should have a clear deadline to prevent frustration.

Be Specific

Avoid vague or ambiguous goals. Instead of "I want to get fit," say "I want to run a marathon." Instead of "I want to succeed professionally," say "I want to get a promotion within one year."

Aim for Measurable Goals

To hit the mark, you need a clear target. If possible, put your goals in quantifiable terms. For example, say that your goal is $100,000 in sales within the year or 50 qualified leads within the month.

Get Enough Input

Make sure you do your research. How many resources would you need to make your goals a reality? When you set goals for a team, make sure everyone is involved in the process. Having a sense of ownership and accountability will motivate the team to work harder.

Strike a Balance

Your goals should be both challenging enough to sustain your interest, but within the realm of possibility. If they are too easy, you will get bored; if they are too hard, you will get discouraged. While pushing yourself is recommended to expand your boundaries, going too far can derail you.

Use the SMART acronym as you create your goals:

- **S**pecific
- **M**easurable
- **A**chievable
- **R**ealistic
- **T**ime-bound

How to Achieve Your Goals

Plan Meticulously

Goal setting involves identifying what you want to accomplish, breaking down the process into measurable tasks and objectives, and giving yourself a specific time frame. To avoid getting overwhelmed, break your goals down into smaller chunks.

Say, if you want to read one book every other week, count the pages and divide them into 14 equal parts. This way, you can monitor your progress and work towards your end goal consistently.

The key here is to write everything down. Don't keep it all in your head. Put your goals in a paper planner or calendar. Alternatively, type it into a planning app or spreadsheet.

Remove Distractions

As mentioned previously, your environment has a great effect on you. What and who you surround yourself with determines your ability to achieve your goals.

Your workspace has a lot to do with your focus. If it's cluttered, there's a strong chance your focus will keep slipping. How many times have you started working, only to get the urge to tidy it all up? It is especially hard if your goals are dependent on your ability to focus.

Similarly, if you surround yourself with people dedicated to their work, you'll strive to compete with them. If you join a team with low morale, you may end up losing your motivation as well.

Record Your Progress

Evaluating your progress is a crucial part of goal setting. This makes it easier to identify weaknesses and compensate for what you lack.

Most people get a sense of satisfaction from visual proof that they are closer to achieving their goals. It can be as simple as putting a smiley face on the calendar for each day you exercise.

Or, you can create colored line charts or bar graphs of your progress.

The important thing is that your progress is visible and accurate.

Overcoming Adversity Along the Way

Expect life to throw hurdles in your path. These obstacles help you grow. As you plan, leave plenty of room for self-improvement.

You will go through hard times. It's a given. But they do not mean the end of your dreams. Here are some strategies that may help you overcome obstacles:

Identify Potential Obstacles

Know what you are up against and learn how to deal with them. Don't fear failure, learn from your mistakes instead. Be positive.

Involve Others

Sometimes, you need a little push to achieve success. Your friends and family can help you by providing both encouragement and criticism. Ask for advice from people who have previously taken a stroll down the same path.

Be Your Own Cheerleader

Remind yourself why you want to accomplish your goals. Why are they important to you? Believe that you are capable of achieving your dreams. A negative attitude will hinder you. Manifest. Tell yourself you can and will reach your goals.

Setting goals is the easy part. Anybody can set goals. The hard part? You'll have to work for it. When you're faced with distractions and hurdles, quitting can be extremely tempting.

If you fall off the wagon a few times or have difficulty in reaching your goals, don't beat yourself over it. It's normal to make mistakes or lose momentum. Give yourself some grace, dust yourself off, and then continue with your plan.

Similarly, if you find yourself reaching a goal, celebrate. Reward yourself. It's an accomplishment. Remember, you only hit what you aim for.

Tackling Your Daily Goals

Daily goals are small goals that contribute towards the bigger picture. Get into the habit of doing something each day that will take you closer to the desired outcome.

Daily goals are a contributing factor to a much larger, high-priority end goal. If you're looking to lose or gain weight, you'll have to work out 30 minutes every day. There are no shortcuts.

Better yet, make achieving your goals a part of your schedule. This will hardwire your brain into accepting it as a natural thing. Your goals will become a part of who you are as a person.

Say you want to improve your health by getting 8 hours of sleep each night. This requires having a fixed bedtime and wake-up time. Just keep turning in at 10 p.m. and getting up at 6 a.m. every day, no exceptions (unless you are sick, of course).

Skip the late-night TV marathon and avoid screens an hour before bedtime. Resist the urge to hit the snooze button.

Studies show you only need 21 days to form a habit. Pretty soon, your body will get used to this schedule.

Are you always scrambling at the start of the workday? Start your workday the night before. Before you sleep, take 15 minutes to write down your to-do list for the next day. Then, arrange it according to its priority. This way, you already have a game plan instead of reacting to whatever is in your inbox.

18-Minutes Technique

Our priorities determine our focus and the way we're willing to spend our time. This principle is the main idea of a book written by Peter Bregman titled "18 Minutes: Find Your Focus, Master Distraction, and Get the Right Things Done."

Bregman stated that to accomplish your goals, you need a ritual. All it takes is dedicating 18 minutes of your day.

What are the key takeaways from this book? How does it apply to daily life?

Key Concepts of the 18-Minutes Technique

Focus on the Best Course of Action

Do you feel stressed by your to-do list? Instead of worrying, pause and reflect on the best way to accomplish your daily goals. It may not be the first thing that comes to mind, so don't be too hasty with your decisions. That pause can spell the difference between a bad day and a great one.

Choose According to Your Strengths

We've all suffered from option paralysis. It's difficult to make a decision when the possibilities are endless. To simplify the process, narrow your choices down to goals that align with your strengths.

Ideally, you should pursue something you're already passionate about. It's easier to devote hours to something you enjoy. Chances are, you already have the skills and the interest to make this happen.

Don't focus too much on your weaknesses or worrying about the future. Instead, spend the majority of your time on things that you value. Often, your passions match your values: family, professional success, or financial independence. When you do this, everything will run more smoothly.

Set Boundaries and Avoid Distractions

You may have an idea of how you want your day to look, but once your attention is diverted, that all goes down the drain.

That's why you need to protect your productive hours. When you dedicate a specific time slot to complete a task, it becomes your deadline. You have to complete the project before the end of that time frame. This means you avoid anything that threatens it.

Set your phone to silent, make sure you have a neat workspace, and get to work. Communicate clear boundaries with your colleagues about interruptions and privacy. This is especially important if you are working from home.

With the 18-Minutes Technique, you don't have to worry about being efficient with your goal-setting skills. Instead, this method tells you to focus on what you want the most and discard the rest.

How to Do the 18-Minutes Technique

Step 1: Morning Minutes (5 minutes)

As soon as you clock in, go through your to-do list and focus on the priority tasks. You must identify tasks that will make your workday highly successful, and separate them from busy work.

After careful consideration, pen in the selected tasks in your calendar. Doing so would give you a rough idea of where and when each task will happen. Because you now have a deadline, it will be easier to see these through.

If you can't fit them all in your schedule, leave out the low-priority tasks for another day.

If something has been on your to-do list for more than 3 days, make sure it is allotted a slot in your calendar. Otherwise, remove it from the list altogether.

Step 2: Refocus (1 minute every hour)

A normal workday lasts 8 hours. Set a timer to go off at an hour's interval for the duration of your working hours. Checking and re-evaluating your progress every hour will keep you on track.

Once it beeps, take a deep breath, and recollect what you've done in the past hour. Has it been according to your schedule?

Did you get anything productive done? Hold yourself accountable for how you spend each hour.

If you've lost focus somewhere in the middle, see where you went wrong and make sure it doesn't happen in the upcoming hour. In a way, this is like the Pomodoro Technique.

Step 3: Evening Minutes (5 minutes)

At the end of the day, spend 5 minutes looking back at what you've accomplished and what you've not. Review how you spent your work hours. Were you able to focus on the task at hand or were you distracted? If so, what were those distractions? How can you ensure it doesn't happen again?

Our environment greatly impacts our productivity. For example, you may get distracted by ambient noise. Your office may have an open plan, or your home may be near a busy road.

You can lessen the impact on your productivity. Buy noise-canceling earphones if you are in an office. If you work from home, consider moving your laptop to an inner room in your house. The noise may seem unavoidable and beyond your control, but don't settle for the status quo.

Time is finite. It is important to use it wisely. You don't want to look back and think about all the things you could have accomplished if only you managed your time well.

According to Bregman, you don't have to do everything you set out to do. What is important is that you did all the things that were important to you. The 18-Minutes Technique can make this possible.

Domino Reaction Technique

This method is expounded by author Amit Offir in his book *24/8 - The Secret for Being Mega-Effective by Achieving More in Less Time*. Offir points out that, in the long run, some tasks offer a greater cumulative payback than others. These tasks create a chain reaction of similar events.

Just like dominoes, you knock down one block, and the other blocks will follow suit. You don't need to touch all of the blocks individually. In practical terms, you only have to put in minimal effort every day to accomplish your overall goal.

For example, if you wrote a bestseller, you don't just get paid for the time it took to write the manuscript. For as long as it sells, you will keep receiving royalties. That amount increases exponentially if your book is turned into a TV series or movie franchise, with the accompanying toys and merchandising.

What does this mean? When possible, choose an activity that you only need to do once, but whose benefits you'll reap long-term. These high-value tasks should be your priority.

Your tasks are your dominoes. Before you start, ask yourself "What's the one thing I can do that will lower the workload of other activities or make it entirely unnecessary?" Establish your priorities and strategies around it.

The same principle applies to habit formation. When you work toward getting better at a certain skill or acquiring the desired behavior, you often activate a positive chain reaction.

Say you want to jog every day. When you started doing that, you automatically started going to sleep earlier too. You also started to lose weight and spent less time watching TV. As you can see, one habit cascaded to a series of more positive behaviors.

If you pay attention, you'll notice similar patterns in your life. Notice how often you check your phone? What started as a way to make life easier has opened the door to a plethora of distractions. That's why you have to be cautious about the habits you form.

Why the Domino Reaction Technique Works

Our Habits and Behavior Are Interconnected

The core idea is that the choices you make in one part of your life inherently affect the other related parts, whether you planned for it or not. It's a given. You're not an exception to the theory of interconnectedness in the system of life.

Consistency and Commitment Are Driving Factors

When your goals reflect your self-image, you are more likely to honor the commitment. If your goals match who you want to be, you'll see them through. That's the beauty of human behavior.

The thing about the Domino Reaction Technique is you don't just build meaningful habits, you also change the way you look at things. It has the power to change your perspective on everyday behavior.

51

The best part about this technique is that you hold the power. You alone determine what changes you want to bring about and how you want them to impact your life.

Here's how you make this work in your life.

3 Key Rules of the Domino Reaction Technique

Start Small

You don't have to go all out. Remember, it doesn't matter which domino falls first. To spark a reaction, you need to pick the task or habit that you're most motivated about. Consistency is key. This will help you form a habit while ensuring you're being true to yourself.

Jump on the Next Task

Do the next thing that motivates you as soon as you're done with the first. The momentum will spur you on. You'll get more committed to the idea of your self-image with each successful "domino."

Do Smaller Chunks

The Domino Effect is all about progress. As long as you're making headway, you're not failing at it. So, if a task looks daunting, break it down into smaller, manageable goals. Just keep it moving. Doing something is better than doing nothing.

If you're not able to smoothly flow from one habit to another, it's probably because you are not observing these rules. Remember, it doesn't matter which domino falls, as long as it is falling, you're doing well.

Decide what outcome you want to achieve and the behavior you're most excited about and work towards it. Give it careful consideration and don't underplay your potential.

Think of each piece of the domino as a desired habit or behavior. When you work on one domino, it will create movement between the other dominoes. Once a domino falls, the others will inevitably follow.

Domino Effect in Organizations

At work, you're a domino. Your potential and output make you indispensable. When you take action for something, your coworkers will do the same.

Your actions not only determine your productivity, but they also have an impact on the people around you and the organization you're part of.

Self-awareness plays a key role. Are you going through something that is bound to cause stress and anxiety? Take a step back and try to figure out why. Identifying the main fear associated with this task helps you gain control.

Through it, you can choose which domino you want to move to trigger the chain reaction. It's all in your hands.

However, the Domino Effect has the potential to have negative outcomes too. Say you miss one deadline. You will consequently miss other deadlines because you haven't seen the first one through.

In a group, this becomes a matter of concern when it hinders productivity on a large scale. If one person is unable to do an assigned task, it can affect the performance of the entire workgroup.

It's a great metaphor to explain what happens in teams and organizations, where both good and bad work ethics tend to cascade.

So, when you incorporate the Domino Reaction in your life, remember that it's a chain reaction. However you deal with a task, it will impact your overall performance.

Getting Things Done Technique

The Getting Things Done (GTD) Technique was created by David Allen. Written a couple of decades ago, it remains a bestselling book in the self-help and productivity category.

One of the GTD principles is that the more things you have on your mind, the harder it is to focus your attention on whatever task needs it the most.

With so many tasks bouncing inside your head, things can get confusing. This is why you spend more time thinking about your tasks than actually doing them. This has the potential to negatively impact your mental health.

According to Allen, our brain is not a storage box; it does a better job of processing information. This method recommends doing a brain dump of all your responsibilities and tasks on a piece of paper or any external system. This way, you'll be able to focus on the right thing at the right time.

Are you someone who gets overwhelmed quickly? Do you find it difficult to segregate and prioritize tasks? Do you have multiple responsibilities both at work and in your private life?

Then this method is perfect for you. If you follow the GTD method down to the T, you can organize your life without stress.

How does the GTD Technique work? It's all about storing, segregating, tracking, and retrieving information.

5 Stages of the GTD Workflow

Stage 1: Capture

The first step can take days to master, and that's okay. After that, it requires writing down every single task, appointment, commitment, project deadline, etc. that's cluttering your head. Start with your inbox.

Choose a system that you can see yourself using every day. It can be as simple as a blank journal or spreadsheet. If possible, get a digital system as it's easy to make edits without making a mess of the entire thing. You can even purchase a GTD app with all the bells and whistles.

Stage 2: Clarify

Now that you have listed down all the tasks, segregate them. Arrange them into a task sheet. See where each of them fits in according to the GDT categories.

Is it doable? What kind of task is it? Is it a high-priority or low-priority task? Arrange it according to the answers you get.

Once you transfer items into a task sheet, remember, you can't put them back into your inbox. Find a place for any additional tasks to fit in days or weeks down the line. If you don't, either trash or archive it.

What about quick tasks? If it takes under 2 minutes to complete, don't add it into the GTD system.

Stage 3: Organize

For the rest, assign all the tasks to a temporary holding tray and process them from there into different categories and systems.

Calendar

This is where all your appointments go. Make sure the date, time, and location are included.

Projects

Anything that takes a length of time to complete and multiple actions to see it through should be put down on a project list that you can access regularly. At work, if multiple people are working towards the same project, write down who is doing what on a piece of paper. This will help you tremendously in the long run, you can take my word on that.

Next Actions

These are items that are not project specific. You can look at and accomplish tasks in this list at your own pace.

Stage 4: Reflect

Segregating the tasks and allotting them a specific time frame does not guarantee you'll see it through. You have to regularly check your lists and review them.

Make sure your systems are up to date. This way, you'll be able to focus on the task you're doing without worrying about potentially missed deadlines.

Reflect on the different categories and systems you have allotted the tasks to and keep checking their progress once a week. A good rule of thumb is to clear out your inbox every day.

Stage 5: Engage

Now that you've listed and segregated your tasks, it's time to do the actual work. GTD has the following criteria for determining your next steps:

Context

Often our work and private lives are intertwined. That does not mean we'll integrate them into one big to-do list as that can be cumbersome. Instead, create a separate list for each context. When you find time on your hands, you can easily browse through these context lists and decide on a task accordingly.

Available Time

Time plays a huge factor. If you have 30 minutes left in your day, you shouldn't pick a task that will take you an hour or two to complete. Check how much time you have available before you proceed to pick a task.

Energy

This is what it all boils down to. Your energy level fluctuates throughout the day. Use it to your advantage. Schedule big tasks and projects around the time you're most alert and active. If you're a morning person, do your most crucial tasks before noon. Night owls are usually more active in the late afternoon and evening hours.

Priority

If you have multiple options to choose from, check their priority status. Always finish high-priority tasks before proceeding to lower priority tasks.

As with any other time management technique, GTD has had its share of praise and criticism.

Strengths of the GTD Technique

Reliability

This system ensures you get your things done on time.

Clear Structure

With multiple lists, this technique helps you focus and complete your to-do list instead of switching from task to task.

Freedom

The GTD method is detailed, yes, but the power lies with you. You alone decide what the best course of action is and what tasks you can see through next. People who prefer detailed instructions may view this as a disadvantage.

Comprehensive Organization

This system ensures you're able to focus on both work and personal projects under a single organizational system. This means that things are less likely to fall through the cracks.

Weaknesses of the GTD Technique

No Prioritizing

The main objective of the Getting Things Done technique is just that: getting things done. You determine which task is more important. If you want to prioritize using the GTD method, you'll have to take help from other apps and strategies.

Complex System

It takes time to master the GTD system. If you skip out on certain facets, you won't be able to avail yourself of the maximum benefits.

No Daily Structure

If you're looking to optimize your goal setting and streamline your daily routine, this technique is not for you. It focuses solely on productivity.

Remember, GTD is not a simple methodology. It requires patience and attention to detail. But this technique has helped thousands of people over the years. If you're looking to maximize your productivity and time, this is a great place for you to start.

Often, people find it difficult to juggle work and home life. If not efficiently managed, you'll end up worrying about your chores while at work and worrying about work while you're at home. This will lower your focus and productivity in both places. This is why it is necessary to build your time management skills.

When learning time management, take baby steps. Introduce it slowly to your schedule. You don't need to go all-in all at once.

So, give one of these techniques a whirl. Soon, you can manage your time instead of letting your time manage you.

Chapter 4 - Time Management and You: Unlocking Your Professional Potential

"Time management is not a peripheral activity or skill. It is the core skill upon which everything else in life depends." - Brian Tracy

Nobody wants to get stuck in an entry-level job. While it may seem comfortable, the boredom and low salary will soon drive you to seek a more satisfying and lucrative role.

It's not just about getting a job that caters to your skillset and boosts your resume. There's a deep fulfillment in reaching new heights in the professional realm.

But don't expect to advance in your career based solely on your educational background and years of experience. Your soft skills also play a huge part in getting that coveted promotion.

The good news? If you are adept at time management, you're well on your way to that corner office.

Why is this skill so important in the professional realm?

The thing is, we're not always productive throughout the day. We have bouts of intense focus and productivity interspersed with breaks and non-essential tasks. This is completely natural. After all, you are not a machine.

But if you want to unlock your professional potential, you need to identify when you're most productive and use this knowledge to your advantage.

It's not enough to work harder and put in long hours. The notion of succeeding by working 60 hours a week and sacrificing everything else is old school. With effective time management, you have the freedom and capacity to work smarter.

Set around attainable goals, time management can have a positive impact on your work output and life.

Benefits of Time Management

Imagine being able to accomplish more without going through intense pressure and anxiety. Not only that, but you also soon gain a reputation for reliability and efficiency. This is possible through effective time management.

When you optimize your day, you reap a ton of benefits. Some of these we've already touched on in previous chapters:

- Increased productivity and efficiency
- Less missed deadlines
- Improved work quality
- Reduced stress
- Less procrastination
- Career advancement and professional opportunities

That's not all! Wondering what other advantages this soft skill brings you in the workplace?

Improved Decision Making

Do you find it difficult to make the right choices at work? When you're overloaded, you tend to focus on completing a task for completion's sake rather than ensuring its quality.

People who cannot manage their time well are often disorganized or shallow in their thinking. They may overlook potential problems and alternative solutions when they feel overwhelmed.

Good time management allows you to make better decisions.

You can devote more time and energy to research and fact-checking before you settle on a course of action. With this skill, you can consider your options with care instead of rushing to make a decision that could impact the entire workforce.

Increased Confidence

People who possess excellent time management skills tend to stand out. They are often the go-to person for high-priority tasks because of their punctuality and integrity.

When you deliver quality work as promised, you draw a positive response from both your peers and seniors. You are heaped with praises and rewards, which makes you feel that you are indispensable to the company.

This professional recognition and validation can give your confidence a considerable boost.

Knowing you're good at what you do gives you the motivation to tackle more challenging projects, which is crucial to succeeding in the workplace.

More Collaboration and Less Conflict

Each individual in a group has different skill sets and temperaments. Since the members of your team possess unique experiences and perspectives, debates on certain topics are normal. When you encourage their input, you may end up with strategies that could yield better results.

This process does not happen instantly. But with proper time management, you have more scope to solicit and consider suggestions and ideas from other team members.

Not only that, but time management can also streamline group work and reduce conflict.

Usually, team members have different tasks in a project. The problem is that one task is dependent on the other. If one person doesn't complete a task on time, it inadvertently affects the performance of the entire team. This can cause resentment and disagreements.

With proper time management, the entire team is equipped to meet deadlines and quality standards. Instead of focusing too much on individual output, the team has the time to communicate and collaborate.

More Learning and Creativity

Lifelong learning is a must if you want to excel in the workplace. It's not enough to have a university degree. Most of the things that you learned in school will probably be obsolete in a couple of years or may not hold you in much stead at your workplace.

If you don't have updated tools or knowledge, you will get left behind. Therefore, it's important to stay abreast of the latest news, innovations, and issues in your field in order to remain competitive.

Also, you need space to reflect and come up with fresh ideas. Productive people usually have time for spontaneity and bursts of creativity. Award-winning campaigns and groundbreaking products are not exclusively the result of hard work; they also spring from deep thinking and inspiration.

However, learning and creativity take a back seat if you are always chasing deadlines.

How can you carve out hours for training, information gathering, and innovation? With time management, it's easy to do so.

Improved Quality of Life

A good work-life balance is probably the top benefit of time management. Contrary to popular belief, your life should not revolve around work. But when you don't have control of your time in the office, you carry that stress back home. You worry over deadlines and performance reviews in the middle of chores or while watching television.

Having good time management skills means you've already scheduled your tasks and have penned in extra time for the unforeseen. This way, you significantly reduce your stress levels, take all the breaks you need, and end your workday on time.

When you're not burdened with work issues, your personal life improves significantly.

Keep in mind that your life outside the office still has an impact on your performance. Due to changes in technology and society, the professional and personal realms are more integrated now than ever before. But with time management, you can be happy and healthy in both areas.

Time Management: It's Possible

Time management can improve your life in all spheres. It's all about prioritizing, scheduling, and managing your hours instead of taking the day as it comes. While spontaneity is good, it's best in limited doses.

Before you go any further, let's quickly differentiate between strategies and skills. These two terms are often interchanged and easily confused, but they are quite distinct.

- A strategy refers to a systematic plan for the future to enhance your performance. Strategies require careful thought, monitoring, and evaluation.
- A skill is a specific learned ability that is required by your job. Each skill is honed and practiced until you can do it automatically.

You *follow* a strategy; you *acquire* a skill. For example, writing reports and bookkeeping are skills. Company policies and programs tend to be strategies.

Managing tasks and scheduling them in your planner may sound straightforward, but these actions need an underlying strategy to guide them. Otherwise, they may not yield the results you seek.

Instead of short-term hacks, learn time management strategies and skills that will help you reach your full potential at work. Let's look at some of them.

Time Management Strategies

Perform a Time Audit

Tracking where and how you spend your hours is key to managing time efficiently.

- Track your time for a week. Write down your activities in 15-minute or 30-minute increments using an app or a paper journal. This way, you have concrete proof of your time expenditure.
- Categorize your activities. Find out how much time it takes to do each activity. Have a weekly total and average.
- Review your time expenditure and see how you can improve on the ways you spend your time.
- Do a time audit at least once a year.

The benefits of time trackers are endless. Time trackers gently push you to complete your tasks and projects. Because you can keep records, you're able to introspect and make changes accordingly.

Choose a Time Management Technique

You don't have to reinvent the wheel, as dozens of time management techniques and methods already exist. We covered some of them in previous sections, including:

- Eisenhower Matrix
- Getting Things Done
- Pomodoro Technique
- 18-Minutes Technique
- Domino Reaction Technique

Each one has rules and tips for maximizing your day. They may differ in the details, but they all share the principle that time is a valuable resource that should be handled with care.

The good thing about these techniques is that you can find one that suits your preference and circumstances. If a technique doesn't work after a trial period, move on to the next. You can also combine or tweak them in a way that works best for you.

Aim for the State of Flow

Have you ever experienced a period when your work seems inspired? Your focus is laser-sharp and the world seems to fade into the background.

You know that you are using your abilities and producing exceptional output.

This total absorption is called a state of flow. You often see it in people playing an intense video game, an athlete during a championship game, or artists in the middle of a performance.

When you are in a state of flow, your perceived expertise matches the demands of the task. It's the complete opposite of boredom, distraction, and anxiety.

To maximize your time at work, strive to reach a flow state. You can do this by:

- Setting clear goals and structure
- Striking a balance between your skills and a challenging task
- Getting useful, immediate, and concrete feedback
- Practicing your skills
- Boosting concentration by removing distractions

When you're in a state of flow, you can produce in one hour what would normally take you most of the day. You barely notice the passage of time; your concentration is that deep.

Prioritize High-Value Tasks

If you are familiar with the Pareto Principle, you know that 20% of your efforts contribute to 80% of your results.

Not only that, but you also only have a limited number of hours to do the work. Think of time as a shelf that can only accommodate a certain number of books. Each book is a task or activity. Given the limited shelf space, you only keep books that you love or find useful.

Therefore, it is essential to identify the tasks that have the biggest impact. Which of them allows you to reach your target faster? Which activities are necessary to produce better results?

Don't forget, being busy is not the same as being productive. If you have an overflowing planner, it does not mean you're doing well, it just means you have a lot of things to do.

But are they really necessary?

Don't jump into the workday without taking the time to orient yourself on these high-value tasks. Otherwise, you may end up wasting the day on trivial tasks. Always ask yourself: Is this activity the best use of my time?

When you're overloaded, complete high-priority tasks first and schedule the less important ones for another day. Ask a coworker for a helping hand. Delegating or outsourcing are also practical alternatives.

Focus on Core Competencies

Do you have too much on your plate? If your job description is writing content, your day should reflect that. If you spend more hours coordinating with other teams or auditing expenses, you won't have enough time for your job.

Before you accept a new responsibility, consider if you are the right person for it.

Also, a task may take up a lot of hours because you lack the skills or tools required. If this happens, invest in the right training and paid apps. The improved efficiency is worth the time and dollars spent.

Know Your Limits

You probably accept that you have a fixed number of hours available. But did you know that you also have a finite amount of brainpower?

Your brain can only process so much information before it starts to get tired and slow down. Your body is not designed to do sustained work for prolonged periods.

Eventually, you will find yourself getting distracted, making mistakes, and losing momentum. Not only that, your temper and health may also be affected. These are signs that your mind and body need a break.

A big part of time management skills is knowing what your limitations are. You could give 100% of your time to work, burn yourself out, and still not accomplish what you set out to do. Make sure you have a fixed start and end to your workday.

Learn to Say No

Do you find it hard to say this simple word? You are not alone. Saying no is tricky, especially in the workplace. Consistently declining invitations or refusing tasks may make you look bad in the eyes of coworkers and superiors.

However, saying no is a key time management skill. You set boundaries firmly, politely, and strategically.

Saying yes to everything may make you popular in the short term, but it is not sustainable. If you fill up your schedule with other people's priorities, you won't have enough time to accomplish your own goals.

Here are some of the things that you can say no to without the guilt:

- Say no to responsibilities that do not fall under your core competencies or job description. This one requires close communication with your supervisor.
- Administrative tasks can be delegated to an assistant or automated using apps. We'll delve more into that later.
- Skip meetings that do not require your input. Ask the organizer to send you the minutes instead so you can offer asynchronous advice.

If you do this, you can say *yes* to:

- High-value tasks
- Professional development
- Exercise and wellness
- Personal relationships
- Community involvement and volunteerism
- Reflections
- Leisure and recreation

It's okay to want to assist coworkers and be a team player, but within limits. Don't bite off more than you can chew.

Automate Tasks

Another strategy is to streamline your day by automating repetitive tasks. Not only do you get them done faster, but these apps are usually less prone to errors.

There's a myriad of free and paid apps that boost your productivity. Some of these tools can be seamlessly integrated with existing office software.

Calendar

It provides you with the big picture of your entire year as well as more detailed hourly blocks. With a calendar app, you can automate reminders and invitations for meetings and other activities.

Email

Explore the functionality of your free email account. Schedule emails, create templates, and filter incoming messages into folders.

Note-Taking

These apps ensure you capture and organize all the information you need for work. Everything is stored in the cloud, so your notes are accessible 24/7 and backed up instantly.

Project Manager

Skip the whiteboard and sticky notes and use these apps instead. These list-based or Kanban-style tools help you identify high-priority tasks, monitor progress, and coordinate with a team.

Time Tracker

Instead of guessing how much time is spent on each task, the app will accurately track each minute for you. If you charge by the hour, this tool is a must.

Distraction Reduction

These block your use of non-essential sites like social media or online news. Some provide music or timers that improve your focus.

Do you prefer pen and paper tools? Using what works for you is perfectly fine. But consider that these automated tools can potentially save you hours each week.

Do Time Blocking

Are you uncomfortable with an overly structured day? Do you tend to multitask? If you said yes to any of these, time blocking may be the strategy you are looking for.

It involves dividing your schedule into time blocks and assigning a block for a specific task. This strategy is akin to monotasking and the Pomodoro Technique. You start by:

- Identify fixed parts of your workday. Usually, these are your break periods, mealtimes, and team meetings. Note the exact time you start and end your office hours.
- Once these are on your schedule, group similar tasks together and assign them to a specific block.
- Instead of ticking off items in your to-do list, look at your schedule and check which task needs to be done. You can only do the assigned task per block.

Here's an example:

8:00 to 10:30 am - Writing

10:30 am to 12:00 pm - Meetings

74

12:00 pm to 12:30 pm - Lunch

12:30 to 1:00 pm - Social Media

1:00 to 3:30 pm - Writing

3:30 to 4:30 pm - Research

4:30 to 5:00 pm - Prep for the next day

Make sure the time blocks cover your entire day. Color code each block if necessary.

Ensure Flexibility

Planning is amazing, but sometimes you have to adjust to unexpected demands. It could be a broken laptop, a blackout, burst water pipes, or a sick toddler. The list is endless.

Life happens, so you need to be flexible. Ensure that you can quickly adapt to unforeseen circumstances to the best of your ability.

A good rule of thumb in the workplace is to under-promise and over-deliver.

Often, your ideal schedule is too optimistic. Even experienced professionals may not have an accurate measure of how long it takes to complete a task.

How can you ensure flexibility in your work schedule?

Make sure your day has margins

Don't fill each minute and schedule too many activities. If your to-do list has more than 10 items, consider trimming it down.

Always have a contingency plan

Make sure that your schedule has enough buffer that an emergency or sick day won't derail your plans.

View your time in terms of weeks, not days

You may not have enough time to do everything important within 24 hours, but you probably can schedule it within the week. A week has 168 hours, which gives you plenty of opportunities to work, spend time with family, exercise, and have fun.

What if everything goes according to plan? What happens to all that extra time?

That margin then becomes the space you need for creativity and spontaneity.

You may be afraid that you will fall into the trap of Parkinson's Law, where the work expands to consume the allocated hours. However, you can avoid this by having a list of quick, fun activities. Pick one as a reward when things run smoothly.

Time Management Skills

Several skills fall under the umbrella of time management. When you master these skills, you will see a noticeable improvement in your productivity.

Some of these soft skills include:

- Making lists
- Prioritization
- Delegation

- Estimating time
- Getting organized
- Time mapping
- Eliminating distractions
- Monotasking
- Goal setting

Here are more skills that will help you reclaim lost hours and deliver consistent results.

Planning

Planning is the key to time management. Without it, you react to situations as they happen. This haphazard approach can quickly sap your energy. Not only that, but you also commit more mistakes and waste time on unnecessary tasks. Soon, you will feel overwhelmed, incompetent, and helpless.

A plan allows you to complete tasks in a controlled and proactive way. You can devote more energy and hours to the things that produce the best results. Since you have a clear direction for the day, it's easier to avoid procrastination and ignore distractions.

Planning doesn't have to be fancy or complicated. Here are some tips you can follow when planning:

- A simple yet effective way to plan is to write down your priorities daily and weekly. This ensures that everything is covered.
- Try planning your day the night before so you can immediately start working as soon as you're at your desk. It should only take you 15 minutes.

- Assign high-value tasks to yourself during the best part of your day. When are you most alert? If you are a morning person, schedule priorities before noon.
- As soon as you write down the tasks you have to complete on a workday, arrange them priority-wise and follow this order. Not all tasks have equal weight.
- Make sure you include a weekly review so you can see your completed and unfinished tasks. Find out what kept you from completing them. This way, you can improve your process.
- Don't be too attached to your plans. Be ready to adjust to hurdles and unforeseen changes. Always have a buffer time.
- Don't say yes immediately. Consult your calendar before taking on additional commitments.

If you are uncertain about priorities or if your job has changing requirements, ask your boss which deliverable is more important. Eventually, you will develop an instinct for structuring your day according to your priorities.

Utilizing a Calendar

Do you feel like you have no control over how you spend your office hours? Are 24 hours not enough to do everything on your list? Both situations can be avoided when you use a calendar well.

Having a calendar is the cornerstone of time management. It offers a wide and detailed perspective of your most valuable resource. Since it is a visual reminder of your daily, weekly, monthly, and yearly goals, you avoid the trap of trying to do everything at once.

Here's how you can maximize a calendar:

- Organize your day based on your priorities and to-do list.
- Plan for recurring events and projects. You are less likely to cram a quarterly report or miss an anniversary if it is already marked down.
- Avoid incurring late fees and penalties by including bills in your calendar.
- Add automatic alerts and reminders.
- Track your habits and monitor your progress.
- Don't forget to include birthdays and fun activities in your calendar. Celebrating these will make your team more cohesive and encourage positive interactions.
- Make sure you set aside time for vacations and regular breaks. If possible, have a weekly rest day.

If you are tech-savvy, take advantage of your smartphone's calendar or an app. You can also use a spreadsheet or paper planner if you prefer.

Streamlining Meetings

Meetings have a place in the office setting, especially for team projects. For example, your boss may wish to discuss a potential client and their requirements. It is often faster to delegate tasks and address issues in person.

However, meetings are usually seen as tiresome and a waste of time. Attendees find them counterproductive when they are:

- too long
- disorganized or rambling
- unnecessary

- monopolized by a few individuals

The worst part? Meetings often interfere with core tasks. They take up a significant chunk of your office hours, which could have been better spent on actual projects.

Before you schedule a meeting, ask: Would an email be sufficient?

For essential meetings, follow these tips:

- Start and end on time.
- Keep it short and sweet.
- Send an agenda to the participants ahead of time.
- Invite only the people who need to be there.
- Have clear goals and concise discussion points.
- Leave the meeting with clear next steps and instructions.
- Try to avoid follow-up sessions.

Decline attending meetings that don't contribute to your end goal or project. Talk with your manager and see if you can sit those out.

How to Stay Productive at Work

Imagine completing everything on your list. Peak productivity is possible, but hacks are not enough. You can't achieve this overnight with a few clever shortcuts.

We've outlined below productivity tips and habits that can help you become your best self at work. Even small changes can dramatically boost your level of productivity.

Find Purpose in Your Work

We're more motivated to perform tasks that hold meaning for us. You've probably heard of the story of the bricklayers interviewed by Christopher Wren. When asked about their job, one said that he was supporting his family.

The second replied that he was constructing a wall.

The last one boasted, "I am building a great cathedral to the Almighty."

Which bricklayer do you think is more productive? Having a clear sense of purpose and a long-term perspective will motivate you to greater career heights.

For the sake of your physical and mental health, it's crucial to pursue what you're interested in. When you do that, you'll be able to enjoy doing your tasks. If you are engaged in your work, you pay more attention to it and achieve peak productivity. Do things that make you happy.

Are you in a job that you don't enjoy? If there are no other opportunities available, remind yourself that your work benefits others. It may seem tedious at times, but you're contributing to the greater good.

Keep Your Goals in Mind

Having clear goals can drastically boost your productivity. The key to ignoring distractions is knowing why you want to stay focused.

It's not enough to have individual or team goals. You need to remember your organization's vision and mission. When you can see the big picture, you understand how and why your work matters.

Identify Your MITs

Productivity experts recommend doing the Most Important Tasks (MITs) first thing in the morning. Don't be tempted to do smaller tasks first. Crossing things off your checklist is a satisfying experience, but it's not the wisest course of action.

By the middle of the day, you have less energy and focus. By the end of the day, you probably have the attention span of a goldfish. That's the worst possible time to do high-priority tasks.

This is why we need to plan our schedule for the day around MITs as it's extremely crucial for productivity.

Wake Up Early

Waking up early has numerous benefits. You have fewer distractions early in the day, so you can concentrate better. By the time your colleagues get to work, you've already finished your MITs.

Set your timer 15 minutes earlier every day and watch how drastically it can change your life.

When you decide to try this out, remember - do not compromise on how much you sleep. Adults require 7 to 10 hours of sleep every day. Otherwise, you will be tired and sleepy the whole time you are at work, which defeats the purpose of the exercise.

Just Get Started

Sometimes, you might find it hard to start a project. It could be because it's boring or intimidating. You end up procrastinating, making up excuses for not doing the work.

The thing is, we cannot control these factors. If you wait for motivation or inspiration to come, you may end up missing your deadline.

Do yourself a favor and take that first step. Then the next. You will soon find yourself in the "flow state" of productivity.

Limit Your Phone or Email Access

Do you check your phone first thing in the morning? Stop this habit if you want to be more productive.

Checking your phone right after you wake has the potential to derail your day. The amount of information that hits you interferes with your ability to prioritize. Instead of following your plan, you end up reacting to what you see on social media or your email inbox.

While it's a great way to catch up with your pals or check your work emails, schedule it for another part of the day. If possible, turn off your notifications and alerts. Just check your email once at midday and an hour before you go home.

By dropping this habit, you start your day on a proactive note. When you do that, you will be more mindful, instead of letting social media dictate your mood and actions.

Set Communication Boundaries

If your workplace layout is open, it's easy to get distracted by colleagues walking around. Dropping by to say "hi" is all fun and games until it becomes a 30-minute-long chat session.

When someone approaches you in the middle of an important task, kindly ask them to stop by at a later time.

However, don't completely isolate yourself from your colleagues. After all, interpersonal relationships are also important in the workplace. You just need to be clear about your limits.

Avoid writing long-winded emails. Use bullets and action points as much as possible. To save even more time, prepare templates for messages that you frequently send.

Pick Up the Phone

Here's a surefire way to save time: ditch the email and dial that number. Call your superior or peer and speak to them about your concern.

Writing takes more time and effort than speaking. Plus, you avoid miscommunication with a direct call. Your tone, volume, and speed all ensure that your message gets across clearly.

Take Time to Recharge

Stop thinking lunch is the only break that you should take to optimize your workday. If you're working on longer tasks, you're bound to lose focus and give in to distractions. Take short breaks, not more than 5 to 10 minutes each time.

Go for a walk, eat a salad, listen to your favorite music - whatever helps you get your groove back. Remember, your brain needs rest so factor the breaks in your schedule whenever possible.

Put Your Phone on Airplane Mode

Social media has glorified staying in constant communication with the people you love. The fear of missing out pushes you to be updated with whatever is happening in the world.

Perhaps you are tempted to check every notification and reply to every direct message and email. In a work scenario, this can be a productivity killer. Those minutes can cumulatively take hours off your work week.

Unless you're expecting something important, put your phone on airplane mode. If you're anxious about cutting yourself off from the outside world completely, put your phone on "Do Not Disturb" mode.

You can select a few contacts that can reach you at all times. Your boss, spouse, and children should be on this shortlist. Use a website blocker app that locks you out of the phone if you still have trouble focusing.

Sustain Your Momentum

If you want to achieve something, work for it every day. It doesn't have to be something big, as long as it's contributing to further your goals.

For example, if you're looking to run a marathon, go on a practice run every day, weekends included. A short break can be detrimental to the progress you've made so far.

Learn to Let Go

Sometimes, quitting can be the best solution. If you can't do a task, don't try to prove everyone wrong and cling to it the entire day. This is probably not the only task on your list.

Focusing all your attention on that problem task will hinder the progress of all the other tasks on your calendar.

Are you stuck? Try coming back to it later. If you still can't get the hang of it, delegate or outsource it.

Get Ideas Out of Your Head

If you have any ideas or inspiration that could be used for other tasks, write them down. Remove these distractions from your mind so that you can focus on what needs to be done.

Always keep a pen and paper on hand - or you can just log them into the notes app on your mobile device.

Experiment with other apps where you can jot down your thoughts, ideas, to-do lists, etc. As long as you don't divert to social media, these apps can contribute to your productivity.

Be Introspective

Introspection is necessary if you want to get better at productivity. Hold yourself accountable.

Ask yourself if you've made significant progress. If not, what's hindering you? Locate the root cause and try to solve it.

Reward Yourself

Every win, however small, deserves recognition. Whenever you find yourself at a loose end, remind yourself of all that you've achieved so far.

Every milestone completed deserves a reward. This can help you to stay focused and motivated.

To Sum Up

At the end of the day, time management skills require constant practice and consistent follow-through. Keep at it no matter how difficult or daunting it may seem and you'll be all the better for it.

Chapter 5 - Best Productivity and Time Management Tools

"For every minute spent in organizing, an hour is earned." - Benjamin Franklin

It has been over a decade since we first heard the tagline "There's an app for that." Since then, this marketing campaign has become a reality. With a few swipes, you have access to thousands of mobile apps with an amazing range of functionality.

Not surprisingly, there are apps designed to make managing your personal and private life easier. Given the wide range of choices, how can you select the best app?

The quickest way to choose an app is to download a free version of the top-ranking app, then give it a whirl for a week or so. There's no substitute for firsthand experience.

What to Look for

Here are factors to consider as you browse through the App or Google Play Store:

All-in-One or Single-Feature

Some apps are designed for a single function while others are more versatile. Apps with one specialty tend to work better than multipurpose apps. However, you may prefer to have all your information in one app. If you have the required technical skills, you can connect different apps using APIs.

Reliability

Remember that you'll be storing important and time-sensitive data on your app. That's why you need to read customer reviews and recommendations. If an app has loads of bad reviews, better skip it.

Native Mobile App

Our lives revolve around our mobile phones, so make sure the tool has a native iOS or Android version.

Cost

Find out if the features and functionality offered are worth the cost.

New vs. Old

Early adopters enjoy trying out the latest software, especially since they have innovative features. However, if the company does not stand the test of time, you would have to shift to another app. An established brand may be a safer bet. Keep in mind that older apps may accumulate unnecessary features over the years, which could slow them down.

User Experience

During the trial period, take note of the following:

- Are the features simple, intuitive, and effective?
- Do you like the color scheme and font?

The app should be easy to use so that you can make it a part of your day.

Top Apps for Productivity and Time Management

Calendar

Online calendars make it easier to create and maintain a schedule. With this app, you can remind yourself and others about upcoming tasks, events, and meetings. The great thing about calendar apps is that you don't have to painstakingly type in or write down each detail. You can also view and compare different time zones. This is a boon for frequent travelers and those who coordinate with people in other countries.

Google Calendar

You can create multiple calendars through the app by signing in with your Gmail account. The best part? It integrates with just about every application available on the market.

Microsoft Outlook Calendar

A big benefit of using Microsoft Outlook is you can integrate your Word, PowerPoint, and Excel files into your calendar. However, the mobile version is not half as good as the desktop app. If you want access to more features, you need to pay for a monthly or yearly Microsoft 365 Personal Plan.

Timepage

If you're particular about the look and feel of an app, then this is the tool for you. Designed by the makers of the Moleskine notebook, Timepage has an elegant interface and a simple layout. It provides features like time tracking and a heat map. The latter allows you to see which days are packed and which are more available.

Email

What will we ever do without emails? They have become the primary means of communication for most companies. Some people even treat them as to-do lists. You must manage them well, as a cluttered inbox can hinder productivity. Thankfully, some apps let you filter, schedule, and track emails without the fuss.

Edison Email

This free app supports Google, Yahoo Mail, Office 365, AOL, etc. The smart notification feature allows you to mute certain senders. It also has a handy bulk unsubscribe feature. This app even lets you track packages and updates you on flight delays, car rental updates, etc.

Front

An email app designed for teams, it lets a group of people access and manage an inbox together. Users can delegate tasks to a specific individual and keep tabs on progress. This prevents duplicates and keeps projects on track.

Boomerang (Gmail)

If you need help tracking your messages but don't want to invest in a full-scale email marketing tool, this is a great add-on service. It lets you schedule a delivery time for your email, then sends alerts if a recipient doesn't reply. The app also has

"Inbox Pause," which helps reduce distractions from incoming messages.

Note-Taking

With this app, you can take down important information and sync your notes across all devices. Make to-do lists, insert pictures, or keep a record of anything you want. Some of these apps allow you to forward notes via email.

Evernote

It helps you keep and organize all your ideas in one place. You can create folders and categories to sift through different types of information. Evernote allows users to edit text, images, files, and audio files. The premium version can be quite expensive, so check if the free app is enough for your needs. It is compatible with Android and iOS.

Bear

This app formats text as you type so you don't have to wait to see what your notes will look like. It also has a useful archive feature that enables you to take a note out of search without deleting it. It is only available for macOS and iOS operating systems.

Ulysses

This tool is perfect for writing long-form content like essays and detailed research, thanks to its hierarchical design. You can publish your notes from Ulysses to WordPress. Like the Bear app, Ulysses is only available for iOS and macOS.

Project Manager (PM)

Are you managing a team? Does your job have a lot of moving parts and changing deadlines? With PM apps, you can efficiently plan your projects, improve scheduling, and delegate tasks. You can quickly integrate new members into a project, even if the team works remotely.

Trello

This app works like a virtual whiteboard where you can create cards and move them from one swim lane to the next. Create multiple boards to keep track of everything, from projects to minute details. Trello is compatible with both Android and iOS devices.

Asana

Here you can create tasks and share them with your team. Everyone in the team can see updates in real-time and track progress. You can see who's working on which task and find out what needs immediate attention. Subscribers can choose from individual and team plans.

Wrike

This tool simplifies the planning process and streamlines the workflow. With it, users can customize reports, dashboards, and forms. They also get advanced insights via performance rating tools, resource management, and more. Wrike can be integrated with GitHub and Adobe.

Time Tracker

Time trackers give you a better perspective of how you spend your time, making them essential for managing your hours.

You can't plan your schedule if you don't know exactly how much time is required for each task.

ProofHub

This app offers powerful features and a user-friendly interface. Aside from being a great time tracker, ProofHub is also an online project management software. It is an excellent tool for people who bill by the hour. As soon as you start working on a task, ProofHub starts an automatic timer. You can also make manual entries. These data entries are stored in TimeSheets, which can be used for invoicing purposes. To do this, you need to integrate ProofHub with other third-party apps. It's available for both Android and iOS.

Clockify

Clockify is a free app catering to both individual users and teams. It's available on Android, Mac, Windows, and iOS. Just like ProofHub, you can manually add the hours or use an automatic time. Clockify also allows you to run weekly reports and summary reports. If you work in teams, you can gain access to additional features by opting for one of the four paid plans available.

Forest

This app makes it interesting for you to focus on the task. As soon as you set a time, you're not allowed to check your phone. During that time, a tree will grow. If you exit the app, the tree dies. Your main goal is to create a virtual forest, hence the name. If you want to plant real trees, there is a paid tier available. You can also track screen time and compete with friends and family.

Habit Tracker

To get better at time management, it's crucial to form habits that lead to this skill. This is where habit trackers come in. Habit trackers enable you to become more mindful of your behavior and encourage accountability and consistency.

Momentum

The tracking features of this app are straightforward. It allows you to export your data to a spreadsheet instead of just holding it in your iCloud, making it easier to track your progress cross-platform. You can also set goals and take notes with this app. However, it's only available for iOS users.

Habitify

If you've got a thing for aesthetic-looking apps, this one's for you. Tell the app what you want to track, and it will send you reminders several times a day. It also provides access to performance data and patterns, making it easier to stick to your goals.

Strides

What sets this app apart is the flexibility it gives you to track your habits. You can set streak goals or take up 30-day challenges. Instead of daily exercise, you can set the frequency to thrice a week.

Distraction Reduction

We're faced with distractions that greatly impact our productivity. A good thing then that distraction reduction apps exist. Say, "See you later!" to any site or app that would affect your concentration.

Freedom

Freedom, unlike a lot of apps on the market, blocks distractions across all devices. Set up blocklists and start a session. It has a lockdown mode that makes it impossible to edit blocklists when your session is active. You can also listen to ambient noises while you work. It's available for iOS, Android, Mac, Windows, and Chrome.

FocusMe

FocusMe is a multipurpose app. It has time tracking, website blocking, Pomodoro support, and scheduling in one nifty package. FocusMe allows you to block specific apps and sites for a certain time or forever. Like Freedom, it has a lockdown mode that blocks you out when you try to access distracting sites.

RescueTime

RescueTime monitors all the sites you use and how much time you spend on each one. You can classify them along the Productive/Unproductive scale. Users can block the sites that distract them the most.

Why Use Pen and Paper

Sometimes, technology isn't always the best choice. For some people, a pen and paper system work best for managing time and productivity. When you use pen and paper, you have a physical record that can be accessed at any time. From printed calendars to bullet journals, there are a lot of options out there.

Advantages

- No need for batteries or electricity
- When you write, you remember things better
- Because you can't open apps, you won't get distracted

Disadvantages

- You can't make edits without making a mess out of your notes
- You have to write copies by hand
- Your notes do not have a backup

An example of a pen and paper system is the bullet journal, a personal organization tool developed by Ryder Carroll. It lets you collect and sort reminders, schedules, meetings, to-do lists, and other tasks in one notebook. It's most effective when you color-code the categories so that you can take in all the tasks at a glance.

Gear Up to Work Smart

We've given you a comprehensive list of the best productivity and time management tools out there - and the best part is that most of them don't cost you anything. But at the end of the day, you also need to remember that each individual has their own life and their own set of priorities. An app that works well for your colleague might not necessarily suit your needs. It is important to select the app or tool that works best for you so you can take charge of your time and boost your productivity.

Chapter 6 - Time Management Tips to Try When Working From Home

"Either run the day or the day runs you." - Jim Rohn

The advancement of technology has made it possible for us to do things that seemed impossible a generation ago. It wouldn't be wrong to say that technology has helped revolutionize our lives in all aspects from the way we communicate to the way we shop, travel, avail of various services including healthcare, and so much more. You only have to look around you to understand the inroads that technology has made in your day-to-day life.

Thanks to the internet, you can talk to someone in another corner of the world instantly. It only takes a few seconds to order goods and services online. Your smartphone probably has more computing power than the equipment NASA used to send astronauts to the moon.

How Technology Is Changing the Corporate Landscape

Technology has also changed the way we work. With the introduction of multi-functional devices like the smartphone, laptops, and computers that are not only high-powered but also faster and portable, we have been able to move most jobs out of the traditional office settings into more unstructured and unconventional settings.

Computer technology has made it possible for us to work on the go, work while on holiday, work at the beach, and even work from home.

One of the biggest advantages of modern technology is the ability to work from home. Remote work, also known as telecommuting, is more popular today than ever before. All you need is a laptop and a fast internet connection, and you're good to go.

Work doesn't have to stop during a snowstorm or even a pandemic lockdown. Employees working on the same team or on the same projects can be spread out across diverse geographical locations or time zones and still deliver exceptional output. Businesses now have virtual teams that work seamlessly together without ever having met in person.

But will a remote setup completely replace working from the office?

Going by trends, it appears that most progressive businesses are investing in cloud-based solutions that will allow a seamless transitioning to remote work. Cloud-based solutions are in huge demand since they facilitate a single access point for employees from anywhere in the world. All they need is a strong internet signal.

Work From Home Reality Check

When you list out all the pros, working from home sure sounds like a dream. The commute is ten steps away. Your boss is not breathing down your neck. You can work in your pajamas, or you may even be tempted to not leave your bed at all.

What's not to like? But remote work can be a recipe for disaster if you think you can work at the same pace and in the same manner as you did in the office. Wondering why? That's because when it comes to working from home you also have to account for the following factors:

Distractions Everywhere

Your office has its share of distractions, but your colleagues are less likely to interrupt you in the middle of a presentation or while you are working on a report. How do you avoid the constant interruptions at home? The list goes on and on:

- A delivery person ringing the doorbell
- Never-ending chores and errands
- Noisy pets demanding attention
- The TV tempting you to binge on the latest series
- Kids thinking it's the perfect time to create havoc
- Neighbors dropping in for a chat

Try explaining your deadline to a cranky toddler who refuses to nap or a pet that insists on sitting on your keyboard.

Where Is Everybody?

Isolation is perhaps the worst part of working remotely. There are no friendly chats with your colleagues or face-to-face feedback from your boss. You will probably miss the greetings from the receptionist that signal the start and end of your workday.

Loneliness seems like a minor thing, but even the most introverted person needs social interaction. Having an emotional connection with your colleagues not only boosts your motivation, but it's also good for your mental health.

But how do you build and strengthen professional relationships when you are miles away?

I Can't Hear You

Discussing projects, delegating tasks, and solving problems can all be done via email and videoconferencing. However, such communication isn't half as good as communicating face to face. You miss out on a lot of nonverbal cues that get the message across.

A video call is just not the same as a face-to-face meeting. Add to that slow internet connectivity, unpredictable interruptions, and ambient noise, and communication becomes even more of a struggle.

Too Much Freedom

You know exactly what is expected of you in an office setting. Employees stay in a specified work area, dress in a certain way, and are closely supervised. All that goes out the window when you start working remotely.

You may find yourself confused by the lack of structure. Should you work at the kitchen table or on the sofa? Which task should you do first? Should you finish that email or cook dinner? It can be daunting to make all of these decisions when you work from home.

When Does Work End?

If you work in an office, you usually follow a familiar cycle: home - commute - office - commute - home. Once you clock in the required hours, you are free to leave. Your time at home is solely for rest and family.

When you work remotely, it's more difficult to separate your personal and professional lives. If you are constantly online, there's the subtle pressure to respond to emails immediately. How can you carve out family time if your boss schedules virtual meetings after regular office hours?

These factors can potentially kill your productivity and motivation. That's probably why most people still prefer to work from an office full time.

But what if you are done with the monotony of a 9 to 5 job? What if you hate the idea of staying in a cubicle, wasting your time on long commutes, and attending useless meetings?

That's where work from home seems like a boon. As long as you have a stable internet connection and are focused and determined about getting your work done within a certain time frame, nothing can stop you from working whenever and wherever you want.

Thanks to technology, more professionals have discovered the benefits of working from home.

Perks of Working Remotely

Goodbye, Commute

Millions of people brave trains, buses, and highways to get to work. On average, an office worker spends 25 minutes commuting to work every day. That number can go up to an hour or more if you live in a city with inefficient public transportation or choose to commute from the suburbs.

Getting stuck in a traffic jam is bound to make anyone's day start on a bad note.

With telecommuting, you save hours each week on travel. You no longer have to deal with jam-packed trains, pickpockets, and pollution. Not only that, but you will also spend less on gas money, fares, and car repairs.

However, some people may not see this as an advantage. They may consider the daily commute as "me" time and a clear distinction between their private and work lives.

More Flexibility = More Productivity

When you work from home, you probably still have a daily schedule and expected output. However, you have more control over how you spend your day. This flexibility allows you to finish high-priority tasks during the times you are most productive.

Studies show that employees perform better when they have flexible work hours. They take fewer sick leaves and accomplish more than their office peers.

If your boss permits it, take advantage of the hours when you are most alert and focused. For some people, peak productivity happens in the morning, while others are more energized in the afternoon.

WFH: A Boon for Businesses

Employees aren't the only ones who benefit from working remotely. Organizations also reap the rewards of allowing their employees to telecommute:

- Companies spend less on operating costs like rent, utility bills, and facilities maintenance.
- Companies can hire the best talent even if they are not in the same city or country.
- Employees are more productive and motivated.

Now that you know the pros and cons of this setup, how can you make the most of working from home?

Work from Home Tips to Boost Your Productivity

Stick to a Routine

Routines are good, especially when the line between work and private life starts to blur.

It helps to have fixed hours for work, family time, and self-care. Otherwise, you end up getting distracted from important tasks. Procrastination is a common problem for those who work remotely.

When you're at home, it's easy to lose track of the time you've spent working. You may find it hard to refuse additional tasks and responsibilities. However, doing so is a recipe for burnout.

Your work-from-home routine doesn't have to be identical to your office life. Remember to clock out as soon as your workday ends. You know what this means: no checking your phone or follow-up emails. Soon, you'll have a better grip on a normal workday than you ever did.

Communication is Key

Working remotely means you now have multiple ways to connect with your team. You need to learn how to use these collaboration tools: emails, video calls, chat apps, project management software, and so on.

What if you need to clarify something urgent with your boss? Pick up the phone and make that call. But make sure your day is not consumed by virtual meetings.

Feeling lonely? Isolation doesn't have to be a deal breaker if you are working remotely. Schedule meetups with people every couple of days. You can also try working from a coffee shop, public library, or coworking space.

Your House, Your Rules

Family members may think you are always available when you work from home. Don't let them get in the habit of interrupting your workday.

Make sure you set clear boundaries with your parents, spouse, or kids before you clock in. Share your schedule and agree on the hours that you can do focused work. If you have a home office with a door, close it when you are on a conference call.

Accept the reality that it is impossible to concentrate on work when you are taking care of very young children. Invest in childcare, as it can make or break your work-from-home routine. If you have a limited budget, you can get help from relatives or friends. Another option is to split the workday so that one parent works while the other focuses on the children.

Remember Parkinson's Law? Keep in mind that chores can also fill your entire day. Instead, set aside a schedule when you can attend to these chores and errands. Once you're in work mode, ignore the laundry and dishes.

Set Up a Home Office

Our workspace has an impact on our productivity. Find a place that's significantly quieter than the rest of the house and has good internet connectivity. Place everything you may need on your work desk, and make sure you remove all possible distractions.

Resist the temptation to work from a bed or couch. Otherwise, you may end up with a headache and a sore back. There's a reason offices invest in ergonomic desks and chairs.

Utilize Your Commute Time

What can you do with all the hours you saved on your commute? Now's the time to create new habits and strengthen existing ones. Your loved ones will also appreciate having more of your attention and presence.

Do you find yourself getting restless? Devote more hours to a hobby, tackle a home improvement project, take a walk in the park, read a book - whatever makes you happy. If it won't affect your main job, find a side hustle that you enjoy. A little extra income can go a long way.

Hold Yourself Accountable

With great power comes great responsibility. If you do not want your productivity to take a nosedive, resist the temptation to procrastinate. Familiarize yourself with all the excuses for rescheduling tasks to a later time. Each time they come up, remind yourself of your professional goals.

Are you finding it hard to stay motivated? Celebrate and reward every small win and milestone you've reached.

Remember, be kind to yourself. Working from home can be tiring, especially if you sit at your desk for hours at a stretch. Make sure to have enough sleep, regular breaks, daily exercise, and healthy meals. During the weekends, try to unplug from any screens.

How you deal with working from home is entirely in your hands. You can make it a fun and rewarding experience or a dull one. The choice lies with you.

Chapter 7 - Talking About Time Management and Time Management Activities

"The key is not to prioritize what's on your schedule, but to schedule your priorities." - Stephen Covey

Imagine that your boss asks you to write a report. Does that mean a one-page summary or a 20-page white paper? If you don't have a conversation about expectations, both of you will end up frustrated.

In an ideal world, managers should be able to understand and explain:

- How much time it takes to complete each task
- Which high-value tasks should be done first
- The criteria for evaluating your work
- How individuals contribute to the overall project
- Ways to troubleshoot issues and adjust to the unexpected

Instead, this is what usually happens:

- Managers set goals and delegate tasks to their subordinates
- The team accepts these without question or complaint

Sometimes, the team fails to deliver on time because they are unsure about the expected output. They may get overwhelmed by changing requirements or increasing workloads. Or, the team may meet the deadline but at the cost of their physical and mental health.

Is this truly the best way to do things?

You may have tried looking for answers yourself but gotten overwhelmed by the sheer volume of content about time management and productivity. Visit any bookstore and you will find hundreds of books in the self-help genre.

A quick online search is not much help either. Typing in "time management strategies" would yield millions of results. Plus, it's not a good idea to blindly follow the latest trend or influencer post. What may work for some may not work for you.

So how can you improve your time management skills? The best way to figure this out is to initiate a dialog with your boss or team.

Why We Need to Talk About Time

Communicating with the people around you is the next step to mastering time management. After all, this skill does not happen in a vacuum. How you allocate your hours will impact your team, family, and community.

Time management is essential, but we rarely talk about it. We are not intentional about discussing or clarifying expectations for spending time at work.

When we fail to talk about time management, we end up with false and harmful assumptions about productivity.

For example, there's a tendency to romanticize hustling and overwork. We glorify neglecting our well-being and relationships for the sake of meeting unrealistic expectations at work. If you want to take time off to rest or attend to personal matters, it's seen as a lack of ambition or commitment.

But what good is working 60-hours a week if you end up stressed, depressed, and burnt out?

How can you have an effective conversation about this crucial topic? It's all about asking the right questions.

4Ds of Time Management

Managing your time involves quick, strategic, and proactive decision-making. Don't make decisions on a whim. Instead, follow the 4Ds of Time Management:

Delete or Drop

You can get rid of unnecessary items by making a judgment call:

- Is it worth your time and effort to do this task?
- Does it contribute to your goals?
- What are the consequences for failing to deliver this on time?

Comb through your to-do list. Sometimes, we do things out of habit or peer pressure. Find out if that meeting or email is necessary. You may be surprised to discover that a task is already being done by another colleague or department.

Remember, deleting tasks from your to-do list should make your life easier, not more stressful.

If you can't remove a task, consider if you can diminish or reduce the time spent on it instead.

- Is there a faster way of doing this task?
- Can you eliminate certain steps in the process?
- How can you automate it?

Delegate

It's normal to feel hesitant about delegating. When you assign a task to a colleague, it may seem like you are avoiding your duty. Or you worry that your boss may see you shirking your responsibility.

You can let go of the guilt by asking:

- Is this task part of my job description?
- Do I have the expertise and time to do it?
- Can someone in my team do it better?
- Am I the only person who can do this task, or can anyone do it?

There's a fine line between delegating tasks and projects and giving up your responsibilities. Make sure you don't cross it, even accidentally.

You may be asked to do things outside of your job description, but those should be exceptions and not the norm. If a task is better suited for someone with more experience, ask for help from senior members of your team.

Before you delegate a task, make sure the other person can do it properly. If you must edit or rewrite it, what's the use of delegating? If you're unable to delegate tasks within the team, consider outsourcing.

Defer or Delay

If you find yourself short on time, defer low-priority tasks to a later date. This can help free up your time for high-priority tasks without you having to put in extra hours. Consider asking yourself:

- Which of these tasks require my immediate attention?
- Does it have to start now?
- Can I do this task over a longer period?

Sometimes, you need to defer a current task in favor of something more urgent and important. For example, you may have to delay writing an article for the newsletter so that you can update your website's FAQ about a product defect.

However, make sure you go back to the first task as soon as possible. Otherwise, you'll have an enormous backlog to deal with someday. Keep an eye on the project deadline.

Do

Once you've identified your priorities, take immediate action.

- What are your high-value tasks?
- Which tasks can be done in a matter of minutes?

- Is this task urgent or time-sensitive?
- Does someone need your output to get their job done?
- Did your boss ask you to prioritize this task?

Try to get short yet important tasks out of the way as soon as possible. You don't want them cluttering your head. This will help you build momentum and keep you motivated.

If you're having trouble with a task because of its complexity or a tight deadline, initiate a conversation with your manager or coworkers. Don't suffer in silence.

People deal with time limitations differently. Together, you are more likely to find an effective way to complete the project faster.

Discussion Points for Time Management

Here are some things to consider before you open a dialog about time management.

- What are the demands on your time?
- Are these demands coming from your boss, peers, or subordinates?
- What is your boss's management style?
- How would you describe the working style of your colleagues or subordinates?
- How does your team communicate? Is it effective?
- What time management skills are you good at? Which do you struggle with?
- What are the monthly, weekly, and yearly goals of your team?
- What are your metrics for success?

- Which projects and tasks align with these goals?
- What resources or tools do you need to reach these goals?

Get the conversation going with these topics:

What Time Management Strategies Are You Using?

You won't know if a time management strategy is effective unless you try it. Evaluate your current productivity habits by asking yourself these questions:

Planning:

- How do you spend your time? Does your schedule align with your goals?
- How do you react to sudden changes or delays?
- Which tasks have the biggest impact on your career?
- Which tasks do you enjoy doing?
- What time are you most productive? Are you an early bird or a night owl?

Health:

- Are you getting enough sleep?
- Do you take regular breaks?
- How much time do you devote to exercise each week?
- Do you have a fixed start and end to your workday?
- How much time do you spend with your loved ones?

Distractions:

- What distracts you from work? Do you tend to procrastinate?
- How do you deal with distractions?
- Do you keep paper and pen nearby to jot down ideas?
- Which apps or websites do you need to avoid?
- Do you need complete silence to focus, or do you prefer playing background music?

How Can You Optimize Computer Use?

Time management requires that you have the right tools on hand. Since everything requires the use of technology nowadays, find out if you are making the most of the resources you have at your disposal.

Here's what you need to discover:

- Do you have the right software and tools to get your work done?
- Do you need a free or paid version of this tool? How much would it cost?
- Are your tools and apps up to date?
- How often should you replace your equipment?
- Do you have reliable antivirus and antimalware software?
- Are your important files backed up in the cloud?
- Do you change your passwords regularly?
- Do you know keyboard shortcuts?
- Do you need to learn how to type faster?
- Do you have multiple programs running at the same time?

You may need input from your IT department for some of these questions. Don't be intimidated by all the jargon.

How Can You Learn from Failure?

You need to adopt a growth mindset; the belief that you can acquire and master any skill or characteristic. In contrast, having a fixed mindset will prevent you from learning from your mistakes.

Find out if you have a growth mindset with these questions. You will also gain insight into how well you deal with failure.

- Would you describe yourself as having a positive attitude?
- Do you tend to complain or blame others?
- Do you believe that you are not good at certain things?
- Are you willing to learn new methods, or would you rather stick with what's familiar?
- Are you willing to ask for help?
- How do you react to obstacles, interruptions, or delays?
- How do you respond to critical feedback?
- What prevents you from achieving your goals?
- Was there a way to avoid the mistake? What would you have done differently?
- Who can help or teach you to overcome your weaknesses?
- What is the worst-case scenario?
- What will you do next?

It can be tough to maintain an optimistic outlook when you miss the mark. Don't let failure define you. Reflect on your mistakes, see where you went wrong, and divert from that path.

Chapter 8 - Time Management Tips from Business Leaders and Entrepreneurs

"The bad news is Time flies. The good news is you're the pilot." - Michael Altshuler

It is fascinating to learn how successful business leaders strived to reach their goals, beat the odds, and emerge as winners. In a fast-paced world where competition is fierce, this is nothing short of a Herculean task.

How did they break the barriers? How did they achieve an outstanding level of productivity?

The first strategy that comes to mind is to burn the midnight oil or give up weekends. Building a company from the ground up is one of the most stressful jobs out there. On average, a startup CEO spends 14 hours a day on the job.

But is this truly a wise strategy?

Overwork may seem like the answer, but it does more harm than good. The cost is simply too great - depression, anxiety, stroke, heart problems, and so on. If you treat rest as optional, your productivity and motivation will soon take a nosedive.

The secret is not putting in more hours, it's about optimizing the use of time for a healthy work-life balance. If you want to reach peak productivity without burning out, having effective skills in time management is a must.

Dan S. Kennedy, one of the most admired and renowned marketing advisors, authors, and speakers has this to say: "Productivity is the deliberate, strategic investment of your time, talent, intelligence, energy, resources, and opportunities in a manner calculated to move you measurably closer to meaningful goals."

How do the tech giants, CEOs, professional freelancers, and world leaders get this right? Discover the strategies and habits that allow them to thrive in high-pressure roles.

How Successful Business Leaders Master Time

Start the Day with Passion

"Passion is energy. Feel the power that comes from focusing on what excites you." Oprah Winfrey

How would you prefer to start your day?

A.   Doing something you love
B.   Doing something you dread

Option A may seem obvious, but does your morning routine reflect this? Admit it - you have probably fallen into the habit of checking notifications and replying to emails upon waking. Perhaps you schedule tedious activities or long meetings before noon. It is time to change that.

Do things that you are passionate about first thing in the morning. Instead of looking at your phone or inbox, start with a task that you enjoy like ideation or writing. You will be able to complete your tasks more efficiently if your day starts on a positive note.

Go for a short run or yoga session before office hours. Your productivity and mood will get a much-needed boost from exercise. Richard Branson (Virgin Group), Jack Dorsey (Twitter), and Tim Cook (Apple) get up at 5 am for a daily workout.

For busy executives like Jeff Bezos (Amazon) and Bill Gates (Microsoft), breakfast is the family meal instead of dinner. It is a great idea to connect with your loved ones then, as evening hours may get consumed by meetings or events.

Keep Goals Top of Mind

"Am I doing the most important thing I could be doing?" Mark Zuckerberg

Time is limited, so you always have to ask yourself if you are using it in the best possible way. You have to keep your goals front and center. Don't let yourself be sidelined by distractions or busywork. Be wary of tasks that seem urgent but do not contribute to your final goal.

Your to-do list should match your goals and most important tasks. If you can only do one thing today, what would it be? Devote your most alert and focused hours on that task.

Remind yourself why that particular task is important. Why do you want to do it? Why is it important for your business to exist? When you focus on the *why*, it will be easier to reach your goals and have a successful business venture.

Identify Time Assets and Time Debts

"Time debts need to be paid. Be careful how you choose them. Time assets pay you over and over again. Spend more time creating them." James Clear

The author of a bestselling book on habits explains that tasks fall under two categories:

Assets

At first, these activities take up a little of your time. But if you do these tasks, they free up more time in the future, which you can devote to your priorities. Examples of time assets are automation and delegation.

Debts

These activities take time away from you without freeing up time in the future. In some cases, they create more work for you later on. Examples of these are procrastination, low-quality work, or emails.

How can you maximize this concept?

Create time multipliers

As the name suggests, these processes and tools create more time. Examples include designing your workspace to minimize distractions and setting clear priorities in your to-do list.

Ensure time assets don't turn into debts

Delegating is only effective if you provide enough information and clear instructions at the start of the project. Otherwise, you end up losing time to problem-solving and substandard work.

Steve Jobs was known to save time on applying for a license plate by changing cars every six months. That is an extreme yet effective example of this strategy.

Stick to a Schedule

"It's not what we do once in a while that shapes our lives. It's what we do consistently." Anthony Robbins

CEOs and leaders are often creatures of habit. While their routines vary, they have the discipline and drive to follow their schedule instead of reacting to what the day brings.

Time management begins with identifying tasks and introspecting where your time goes. You need to build a realistic schedule that reflects your priorities and accounts for how much time you require to complete certain tasks.

Design your schedule to take advantage of your most productive hours. When do you find it easier to do deep work? When is it more practical to hold meetings? Which period do you find your energy lagging?

Once you have created a schedule that works for you, follow it. Don't wait for inspiration to strike before tackling your to-do list. If you don't follow a schedule, your productivity will be at the mercy of other people's priorities.

Make Time for Possibility

"It always seems impossible until it's done." Nelson Mandela

Entrepreneurs are known for thinking out of the box. Instead of settling for tried-and-tested techniques, they innovate and imagine. You need to push your limits and do things you've never done before.

That's why you should have enough time in your schedule for creativity and serendipity. If you are too busy, you will fail to get out of your comfort zone. Give yourself time to think, dream, and ask, "What if...?"

Companies like Google, 3M, and Atlassian encourage staff to devote part of the work week to independent projects. About 20% of their paid time can be used to pursue ideas or learn about new trends.

Practice Mindfulness

"Our life is shaped by our mind, for we become what we think." Buddha

Mindfulness and meditation can help improve concentration. These practices allow you to be in the present instead of worrying about the future. You can get more work done when you block out distractions and stay focused on the task you're working on.

Another benefit is that you are aware of where your time is going and how you are spending it. Mindfulness is the complete opposite of multitasking, a productivity killer that should be avoided at all costs.

Review Your Workday

"Evening question: 'What good have I done today?'" Benjamin Franklin

One of America's founding fathers, Benjamin Franklin was an advocate of self-improvement. Franklin developed a daily chart that let him track his goals. This way, he always knew how he spent his day and whether his activities aligned with his goal.

No matter how carefully you plan your schedule, you may need to change it when something else demands your attention. Not having control of your day can make you stressed.

To address this, do a self-review. By the end of the day, ask yourself, "What progress have I made so far?" When you review and understand what you have accomplished in a day, you're bound to feel motivated.

Get Enough Sleep

"Eight hours of sleep makes a big difference for me, and I try hard to make that a priority." Jeff Bezos

Sleeping is not a waste of time. It allows your body and mind to recharge so that you can perform at your best during your waking hours. The number of hours would depend on your unique needs.

Given the demands of the job, executives and entrepreneurs often get by on 6 hours of sleep or less. Examples of these "sleepless elite" are Angela Ahrendts (Apple), Elon Musk (Tesla), Sergio Marchionne (Chrysler Fiat), and Marissa Mayer (Yahoo).

Contrary to popular belief, reaching the corner office does not always mean sacrificing sleep. Bill Gates, Mark Zuckerberg, and Jeff Bezos are just some of the business leaders who have established huge businesses while still getting the recommended 8 hours.

Be Intentional

"We think, mistakenly, that success is the result of the amount of time we put in at work, instead of the quality of time we put in." Arianna Huffington

Time management is not something you stumble on. You may have the desire to succeed, but that's not enough. You need to be intentional about how you spend your hours. Instead of focusing on quantity, consider the quality of your work hours. Take inspiration from successful business leaders and founders who have mastered time management.

Chapter 9 - Choosing Between What You Want Now and What You Want Most-Time Management Habits You Should Consider Developing

"Efficiency is doing things right; effectiveness is doing the right things." -
Peter Drucker

Time management is a crucial skill, one that allows us to be effective about how we spend our time and what we spend it on. When you manage time the right way, you open doors to higher productivity, more control over your day, and improved integration between your work and private life.

It's the most beneficial life skill one can possess.

You only have 24 hours in a day. The idea of getting everything done in such a limited time frame can get overwhelming and stressful.

What do you do then?

Choosing What Matters

Do you prioritize and leave some tasks out, or do you slave throughout the day and make a huge mess of your private life?

Perhaps the reverse is true. Do you take control of your private life but leave your work life in the backseat? What's the solution?

You need to make a decision. You must choose activities that yield favorable results in the long run instead of those that only lead to short-term benefits.

Discipline Is Not a Dirty Word

As Abraham Lincoln said, "Discipline is choosing between what you want now and what you want most."

Nowadays, discipline gets a bad rap, but this quote puts the word into perspective. Don't take it as a criticism, consider this a call to action to make better decisions.

We have limitations when it comes to time. No matter how much we want to, we cannot manipulate time. What we can do is choose to use it wisely.

We all have goals and expectations. When we manage time, we actively choose to run our whole schedule through the machine we call "prioritization."

Which would you prioritize: instant gratification, or success? Instant gratification may feel good at the moment, but it won't help you reach your goals.

When you say, "I don't have time for X," what you're really saying is, "It's not a priority."

Stop Making Excuses

It's easy to see yourself as a victim of unmanageable hours and unrealistic expectations.

"I don't have time to exercise or go to the gym."

"It's impossible to get enough sleep."

"I can't schedule a weekly date with my spouse."

"I want to write a book, but I can't right now."

"I don't have time to prepare or cook healthy meals."

"I need to reschedule my doctor's appointment."

"I have to cancel a spa day with my friends."

"We don't have time to go on a family trip this year."

Your "massive" workload becomes a handy excuse for failing to meet commitments, do basic self-care, or maintain relationships.

Being compassionate towards yourself is not selfishness. You can't pour from an empty cup. Your needs, wants, and goals are just as important.

This is not intended to downplay the struggle people face when it comes to time, but does it truly help to see yourself as a victim of circumstances?

Who's the Boss?

Why not reclaim control over your time and reframe your relationship with your schedule?

Time management is a skill that a chosen few possess. That's not because it is a difficult skill to master. The truth is, most people don't know the habits that aid the process.

No worries. Learning or developing habits is not the easiest route you can take on the road to success. It comes with its own set of hurdles. Once you know what you should work on, you've won half the battle.

Importance of Developing Time Habits

Habits are routine activities that meet essential needs. You probably don't give them much thought. When confronted about your habits, you may find yourself claiming that they simply can't be changed.

"Working out twice a day is a habit I developed over time."

"Smoking cigars is a habit I can't shake off."

"My coffee habit is non-negotiable."

"I'm habitually late to meetings."

"It's a habit to wake up early and meditate."

These are statements we say or hear regularly. But are they true? What actually constitutes a habit?

Let's find out.

Where Do Habits Come From?

Some habits form without a conscious decision, usually based on how things are done in your family of origin. You always have oatmeal for breakfast because that's what you had as a child. You brush your teeth regularly because your parents trained you to do so.

Other habits are adopted without conscious thought, usually because you associate them with fun or a sense of belonging. You always take a certain route while commuting because you've gotten used to it. You started smoking after your friends offered you a cigarette. You need a daily latte because your colleague invited you to a coffee shop.

As an adult, you can also decide to develop habits that you consider useful. Examples are exercising, meditation, quitting smoking, dieting, reading self-help books, etc. These may require more effort at the beginning, but it pays off in the long run.

The best part? Habits, once ingrained, become automatic. You no longer have to give yourself a pep talk to continue doing them. It almost becomes a part of the subconscious.

This can come in handy when you're developing habits to have a better hold of your time.

Habit Formation and Time Management

To be good at time management, you have to learn and develop the right habits. This way, controlling your time and planning your schedule becomes effortless.

Keep your eyes on the goal when choosing time management habits. It's not just about being productive at work or being more efficient at meeting deadlines.

You can be productive and efficient at the wrong things.

Instead, your time habits should help you achieve the priorities you've chosen for your life.

Time Management Habits You Should Consider Developing

Identifying Your Purpose

This is all about keeping your eyes on the prize.

Ask yourself: Why do you want to achieve a certain goal? How will it help your end goal? What lengths will you go to achieve them?

Identify what you want and work towards achieving it. The more clear-cut your goals, the easier it will be to make them a reality.

Do a mental exercise and rearrange your priorities. If you have too much on your mind, jot it down. Make a list of all your goals and then break them into smaller, more achievable tasks. Make sure you work on it every day.

Take baby steps. Trust the process. It's easier to get hands-on with everything when you have your goals all figured out.

Eliminating Distractions

When you set out to work, don't let distractions set your pace and productivity. The thing with distractions? They seem so inconsequential and beneath your notice. However, these trivial things hinder your productivity.

You probably think that it doesn't matter if you spend 5 minutes on social media or 10 minutes snoozing in. But if you add them up, you will find that you've lost hours of your time.

Electronic Devices

Something as small as checking the phone for notifications or replying to a DM can set you back by hours. How, you ask? It takes at least 20 minutes to regain the focus you've lost after an interruption.

It's ironic, really. Phones, laptops, and computers were designed to save time, but they're doing the exact opposite.

What do you do then? Form a habit that eliminates these distractions. Make it part of your routine to put your phone in silent mode or turn off notifications. Set an alarm to check your email only once or twice a day.

Download an app that bars you from using your phone during a stipulated time frame. Better yet, switch off your devices when you need to do deep work.

People

Interruptions from others can be as detrimental to your workflow as your mobile devices. This is true whether you are working in an office or working from home.

Establish personal space and boundaries in advance. Communicate these clearly. You don't have to come off as rude, but let people know you appreciate being left to your own devices while you're working.

If you function better while listening to music, invest in noise-canceling headphones.

When you eliminate distractions, you're able to focus your attention fully on the task at hand. This, in turn, helps you be your most productive self and achieve better results.

Single-Tasking

There's a misconception that multitasking means you're getting more work done. This can't be farther from the truth. This soft skill mentioned widely in resumes is a silent barrier to productivity.

Let's say you have a task that's supposed to take two hours. Midway, your boss gives you another task to complete.

It may be tempting to multitask. Don't. Either you will end up submitting substandard work, or it will take you longer to achieve either task. When you jump from one task to the other, you lose momentum and focus. Focus is something we cannot afford to experiment with.

Taking Care of Your Health

A well-rested mind is a key to improved productivity. Sleep deprivation is not a badge of honor. You need an average of 8 hours of sleep each night. Some people thrive on only 6 hours, while others need 10 hours or more to be functional.

How can you get enough sleep? Give yourself a fixed bedtime. While it's tempting to decompress by watching TV for hours, what your body truly requires is sleep. Make it a habit to go to bed and wake up at the same time each day.

Any time you see yourself losing focus and getting restless, catch a short nap. After waking up, you'll notice that you're more refreshed and ready to take charge of your day.

Make sure you drink plenty of water during the day and eat healthy. Put exercise and recreation in your schedule. Your overall well-being is a great determiner of how well you'll be able to manage your time.

Giving Yourself Deadlines

Setting deadlines can help you battle procrastination. Create a schedule and stick to it. It doesn't have to start super early. Work during the hours you're most alert and energetic.

Soon, you will notice that you get more work done on the days that your schedule is all mapped out. You'll be more motivated, optimistic, and adept at taking on new challenges.

Setting a schedule automatically gives you a deadline. When you have a deadline, you're less likely to procrastinate.

Focusing on High-Priority Tasks

Time management can be tricky. You may schedule a task, work towards completing it, and still not get it done. That's okay, for the most part. Not all days are productive. The sooner you understand that the better.

The only drawback? It impacts the completion of all the other tasks on the schedule. This becomes a problem when you have a high-priority task scheduled later in the day.

Priority tasks are the things you need to do right away. They yield the most benefit for you and your team. When you work with a group, completing a high-priority task can sometimes contribute towards the completion of an entire project.

As much as possible, do high-value tasks in the morning. Mornings are the most productive part of the day - plus people won't have to wait long for your output.

Not a morning person? If you're someone who has random bouts of productivity spread throughout the day, slot in the tasks during these peak periods.

Writing Everything Down

Make your schedule and goals tangible. Write everything down. When you write things down, you're more likely to remember them. Handwritten notes stick in your memory longer than typewritten ones.

Living in a world driven by technology, we don't really understand the importance of pen and paper. It's time to change that. Develop the habit of writing everything down from small tasks to year-long goals.

Taking Action

Writing down lists and creating elaborate schedules is not enough. You have to take action.

Keep your goals and objectives in mind. Only you know the importance they hold for you, so make sure you don't let it slide down the black hole. Keep on reminding yourself and hold yourself accountable.

When developing new habits, make sure you don't exhaust yourself. Don't take on too much too quickly. Choose to develop one or two habits at a time. The last thing you want is to make your life chaotic by making a lot of changes back-to-back.

The Bottom Line

Increasing your productivity does not have to be hard. Develop the habits discussed in this article, and you'll find how incredibly easy achieving your goals can be.

Time management is a boon, one that allows for improved relationships, work performance, and overall health. It's the one skill whose rewards you can reap for a lifetime.

Again, you need to make a conscious decision between what you want now and what you want most. Once you've made that choice, select the time management habits that allow you to reach those goals.

It's not too late to choose.

Chapter 10 - You Snooze, You Lose - Work Less and Play More with These Time Management Tips

"Your future is created by what you do today, not tomorrow." - Anonymous

After reading the previous chapters, you now have all the information you need to manage your most valuable resource. But are you still overthinking and experiencing doubts?

Does time management still seem beyond your reach?

Analysis paralysis is a real thing.

For most people, it's natural to seek loopholes and make excuses when faced with a major decision. No one wants to leave their comfort zone, even if doing so means an improved quality of life.

It's so much easier to coast along and blame your circumstances. But if you truly wish to manage your time well, you need to take action.

Whatever it is, remember - you snooze, you lose.

In a bid to find the perfect solution, we fail to notice what lies right in front of us. People who excel at managing time are not special. They don't possess a rare gene or superpowers that make them time gurus.

What they do have is an understanding of the importance of time management.

The Importance of Good Time Management

Consider time management as a scaffolding for the overall structure of your life. As you pour in the cement - your priorities, schedule, and activities - you'll be glad to have a sound framework.

When done right, time management can change your life. No more trying to focus on several tasks while running on a few hours of sleep. No need to risk burnout and isolation just to succeed professionally.

Before we proceed, let's clear up two misconceptions about time and productivity:

- Multitasking is the gateway to productivity.

- Being busy means you're being productive.

If you look at these misconceptions closely or if you have followed through with them at least once in your lifetime, you know how preposterous they really are!

Multitasking is only good when you're singing your heart out in the shower or when you catch up on the news while doing laundry. But that's as far as it goes. When it comes to working, it's a big no-no. The time it takes to regain focus when bouncing between tasks is just not worth it.

On the same note, you're not being productive just because you're busy. You can spend your entire day being busy while accomplishing nothing important. Having a packed schedule does not equate to being productive.

Now that we've got that clarified, what's stopping you from taking the next step?

Work Less and Play More with These Time Management Tips

The best part of time management is that it can be learned. It's not a skill that's reserved for a special few. Here are some practical tips to help make the most of each second.

Track Your Time

Isn't it a waste of effort to track time? Instead of listing an activity, would it not be better to go ahead and do it?

This task is not intended to make things harder. As any good accountant or auditor will tell you, tracking your resources is crucial.

How do you expect to get better at time management when you don't know exactly where your time is going? How can you address your weaknesses if you don't know what they are?

You need to know how you spend every waking hour to get better at managing time.

Start by jotting it down on a piece of paper or creating a spreadsheet. If you find these too cumbersome, install a time-tracker app. Those work like magic.

You can track your activities in increments of 15 or 30 minutes. Do this for at least a week so that you have an accurate picture of your life. Don't forget to include the weekends.

When you track your time, you automatically become more conscious of the allowances you have been making to your scheduled tasks. This can help you create a workable schedule that results in high productivity and better focus.

Prioritize and Plan

Prioritizing is a skill that allows you to give your undivided attention to a high-priority task. When you get these out of your schedule, you don't have to stress over them while working on other projects. It's a win-win.

Without clear priorities, you won't know where to start. Trying to make sense of the day becomes more difficult. Our workload can sometimes be too overwhelming. Pair it with the demands of your private life, and things can seem insurmountable.

The next time you find yourself in a fix, write all of your tasks down and schedule them in order of priority. Your best bet?

Mornings. No part of the day can compare to mornings when it comes to productivity – unless, of course, you're a night owl.

Employ the Eisenhower Matrix or the 4 Ds of time management to help you figure out the Most Important Tasks (MITs).

Before you sit down to create a workable schedule, make sure you understand the difference between not knowing how to manage your time better and being overloaded. It's possible that you have too much on your plate.

Above all else, make sure your goals are achievable. You don't have to be a one-person army and try to do everything on your own.

Your value and expertise in your career are not dependent on finishing an insane amount of work. What matters is the quality of work you provide. So be smart. Do what you do best, and delegate the rest.

Use Tech to Your Advantage

When it comes to time management, technology can be both a boon and a bane. Is that surprising? Not really. Everything comes with advantages and disadvantages. Your outlook and perspective determine what side you want to focus on.

Tech can be the greatest weapon in your time management arsenal. There's plenty of software and apps available across various platforms: calendars, time trackers, habit trackers, virtual assistants, email automation, and note-taking apps.

Find the one that works best for you. Because these apps take care of more than half of your workload, they can help maximize your productivity. Don't hesitate to invest in a premium plan if the product has the features you need.

Ditch Mobile Devices

After preaching about how useful technology can be, now you're being asked to get rid of your smartphone? This seems the exact opposite of the previous point, but there's a reason for that.

Installing software and apps to facilitate a better hold of your time is good. But you need to balance the pros and the cons of using technology. These flaws can negatively impact your productivity.

Like the majority of smartphone users, you're probably in the habit of checking your phone multiple times a day. You wonder, how much harm can a quick peek on the notification bar do? As it turns out, a lot.

This seemingly minor habit is one of the worst productivity-killers.

Let's not pretend that it only takes a few seconds to check your phone. You know you're not going to play peek-a-boo with the notifications and leave it at that. You're going to reply to that DM and start having a conversation. You'll find yourself clicking on a hyperlink on that blog or sharing that cute meme or cat video. Without realizing it, you've fallen into a rabbit hole of distractions.

See the cycle? That's toxic for productivity.

As soon as you enter a state of flow, put your phone in silent mode. Better yet, turn it off altogether.

Employ the 80/20 Rule

According to Vilfredo Pareto, 80% of the results we achieve are based on 20% of our efforts. Test this formula by applying it to your work routine, and you'll notice how much time you spend on activities that don't contribute towards your end goal, activities you can do well without.

Try to locate the activities that form a part of the 20%, and work on these high-value tasks. These usually correspond with your MITs.

The Pareto Principle helps you stay focused on the things that get results. That 20% is why your company is paying your salary. If you are an entrepreneur or freelancer, it's why your business is up and running.

Employing the Pareto Principles is tough, but the surge in productivity it can offer is undeniable.

Be Compassionate Towards Yourself

Do you want to be a superhero in your workplace? It feels good to be trusted to save the day. But the thing about superheroes is that they're fictional. So why hold yourself up to unrealistic standards?

Know your limits and respect your boundaries. You don't have to always be optimistic, accept task after task, and work on weekends.

Sure, you'll probably get that promotion, but don't be surprised if your family and friends grow emotionally distant. Don't be shocked that your health takes a hit, and you find yourself spending your bonus on healthcare.

Slot in any task you need to complete during the workday. If you're open to taking additional tasks without exhausting yourself, go ahead - but be realistic.

Learn the Power of "No"

This two-letter word holds immense power. Then why won't you use it? In the work setting, refusing to do a task may seem like career suicide. But saying "yes" all the time is just as harmful.

You may think that agreeing to all of your tasks means that you become the go-to person on your team. Who doesn't want a reputation for being helpful and competent? However, if you overcommit and under-deliver, you will soon gain a reputation for being unreliable.

Saying "no" involves a calculated decision. You don't want to decline a task that's both high-priority and urgent. No company wants to be associated with someone who doesn't align with the brand image. Your boss has a reasonable expectation that you are willing to do your best to meet company goals.

To avoid this trap, ensure your manager and coworkers are aware of your workload and schedule. You want to aim for tasks that contribute to goals that yield the best long-term results.

Remember, **prioritize**.

If you can take on additional responsibilities without delaying or performing poorly in your current tasks, then go ahead. If you're a people pleaser who finds it hard to decline anybody's request, tread wisely.

Take Frequent Breaks

Time management means devoting time to rest. Rest is key to having a refreshed and alert state of mind.

People often mistake productivity as being busy throughout the day, taking little to no breaks during our work hours. This can prove to be counterproductive.

Our brain functions nonstop, cycling between high and low focus throughout the day. It's at work even while we sleep! The last thing it needs is overwork.

When you spend more than an hour or two on a project that requires your complete focus and attention, take a break. It doesn't have to be a biggie, 5-10 minutes should be more than enough.

Won't this take time off your working hours? Don't worry. When you put your brain through 8 to 9 hours of constant work, your focus fluctuates. Taking frequent breaks can help solve this problem. When your brain has enough rest, your retention and accuracy get a boost.

Maintain Your Flow

Productivity is linked to being in a state of flow. When your mind is highly engaged in a task, you don't notice the passage of time. You are so absorbed that those distractions don't bother you.

However, this state of flow can be tricky to achieve. There are simply days when you get stuck. You shouldn't let your failure to complete one task determine your productivity for the entire day.

Move on. Start another task and see it through. Establishing a steady workflow is not a small feat, so why lose it over one measly task you can do by the end of the day?

If you don't have any other task scheduled after that, put yourself directly in the path of motivation. Talk to people and figure out a solution. Listen to podcasts and motivational videos - whatever helps you get your groove back on.

Find a Hobby

Work is an important component of our life, but it's not the be-all and end-all of our existence. To truly live and not just exist, we need a reason to feel alive.

Find a hobby or something that helps you recharge mentally. It will give you something to look forward to, irrespective of the kind of day you have at work.

Not only that, but a hobby can also give you an opportunity to explore problems without worrying about failure. Your recreational activities can be a great source of creativity and inspiration, both of which transfer to your professional life.

Hobbies and playtime keep stress at bay. Indulge in as many non-work activities as you can. Make time to pamper yourself every day.

Something as small as a dinner with the whole family or meeting friends at a club for a drink can improve our mood significantly. Make time for play. It does not have to be fancy. Schedule a card game, play fetch with your pet, or chase your toddler around the living room. If it causes you to laugh, that's even better.

Put a Check on Your Habits

Habits can both be good and bad. Once you form a habit, it's difficult to shake it off. That's why it's vital to evaluate and segregate the good from the bad.

If you have something you want to work on for a long period, turn it into a habit. It doesn't have to be work-related, it can be anything under the sun.

Planning to live a healthy lifestyle? Slot it into your schedule and work out at the same time every day.

Developing habits doesn't happen overnight. It takes time, so don't expect to see immediate results. You must not give up. Patience is key.

Work on getting rid of your bad habits. Anything that deters your productivity or negatively affects your lifestyle needs to go straight to the bin. No excuses.

It's much more challenging to stop once a habit gets established. You can't instantly go cold turkey on a decades-long chain-smoking habit. So, avoid getting into the habit in the first place. If you're tempted by anything harmful, nip it in the bud.

The Takeaway

These tips can help you make the most out of your time. Time management is akin to playing chess. You need to understand how each action can have an impact on your overall goal. Both require a grasp of strategy and a willingness to make sacrifices.

Time management is a foolproof way of being in the know, doing your best, and preparing for any obstacle life might throw your way. Life is unpredictable, and you need to be ready for anything.

Take changes in stride and adapt accordingly. Only then can you fulfill the vision and goals you've set for yourself. You may not be able to control the number of hours you have in a day, but you have ultimate control over your choices. Choose wisely.

www.ingramcontent.com/pod-product-compliance
Lightning Source LLC
Chambersburg PA
CBHW071654210326
41597CB00017B/2211